Visualizing The Sermon

A Guide To Preaching
Without Notes

Hugh Litchfield

Hugh Litchfield
Publisher

VISUALIZING THE SERMON

First Edition
Copyright © 1996 by
Dr. Hugh Litchfield

Scripture quotations are from the *Revised Standard Version of the Bible*, copyrighted 1946, 1952 (c), 1971, 1973, by the Division of Christian Education of the National Council of the Churches of Christ in the USA. Used by permission.

Library of Congress Catalog Card Number: 96-94694

ISBN 0-7880-0909-5　　　　　　　　　　　　　　PRINTED IN U.S.A.

DEDICATED

To the memory of
Dr. Linwood T. Horne, Jr.
My "Paul" in the ministry
"He was a 'letter from God' to me"

TABLE OF CONTENTS

PREFACE

To write a book on preaching is a dangerous undertaking. To do so might cause one to think you have an oversized ego. One, for thinking that you can preach. Two, for thinking you can tell others how they can do it better. I make no claim to any such abilities. I feel that no one of us ever learns how to preach. We are always learning and that journey never ends. Likewise, there are so many ideas about how to preach, no one can say that he has found the right way. In this matter, we are all learning from each other.

Then why did I write this book? To be honest, to get some people "off my back." Since I have been able to preach without notes, often after I do, someone will come up and ask me how I do it. I try to explain that it is not as hard as it seems, that I have developed a system to help others learn it. They want to know, "Where is it? Where is it written down?" I would tell them that it was still in my head, and one day, I would try to put it down. Such friends and students have kept after me to write it down for years. They would not give me rest. They pushed, irritated, and encouraged me to do it. Finally, I hope to get some peace from them.

I have decided to use a very informal style in writing this book. I tried to imagine us having a conversation, or being in a classroom as I shared my ideas. If anything, I have tried to be practical, to seek to make it clear and understandable. That will hopefully keep the possibility of preaching without notes within the realm of possibility. I tried to "sit where you sit" and imagine your reactions and questions. I hope I have done that well.

Now I am not coming down from some homiletical Mt. Sinai with a set of unbreakable laws for preaching. What I offer is a possibility. Everyone cannot preach without notes. There are gifted preachers who use notes in some form or fashion. Each of us needs to find the style and system that enables us to be the most effective communicator we can. I am simply seeking to share my thinking and experience. Some of you may have the possibility to preach without notes. I write this book to encourage you to see.

I want to thank the trustees and administration of the North American Baptist Seminary for granting me a sabbatical to finally do this project. I appreciate their encouragement and support. I am also in debt to those students, friends, and colleagues who did "push" me to do it. I am grateful for their confidence that I would have something worthwhile to offer.

I am thankful to Pat Asche, the faculty secretary, who typed the manuscript and put it on a computer and did all those technological wonders that baffle my mind. She is patient and efficient and kind.

To my wife and three children, I thank you for putting up with my "grouchiness" as I tried to meet deadlines. I know it was not always easy. Maybe now, there will be peace.

So I share this book with you. Although it is often said, it needs to be said. Any good that can come from it is due to the magnificent grace of God, who is the giver of gifts, the shaper of abilities, and the source of any worthwhile sermon we could ever preach.

Chapter 1

The Beginning: The Courage To Risk

"I could never do that." Usually this is the response my students give when I suggest that they might preach without notes. To them, it is a terrifying thought. It is hard enough just to stand before a congregation and preach, but to take away the security of notes is unthinkable. They feel like David facing, not one, but a roomful of Goliaths and when they reach down for some rocks for their slings, they have been taken away. So they feel helpless and vulnerable, with no words to help them survive.

I can understand that feeling. It was mine when the seminary professor challenged us to think about preaching without notes. It would be nice, I thought, but you have to be greatly gifted and talented to do that. I was neither of those two and so I quickly dismissed such note-free preaching from my life. But a funny thing happened on the way to developing my preaching. As most of you know, in seminary you have to preach in class before the teacher and your peers. Talk about terrifying! As I prepared to preach my second sermon before them, I was determined not to make the same mistakes which plagued my first one. I prepared diligently for it. I really got to know that sermon. When the time came to preach, I took my full manuscript into the pulpit with me. I took a deep breath and began to preach. Before I knew it, I was finished. Then it hit me! I had not looked down at my notes once. I knew the sermon so well that once I got going, it just seemed to flow naturally and I had no trouble remembering it. I was amazed!

A few days later I was back in Virginia for Christmas and my home pastor asked me to preach. Well, my one good sermon was back in Texas, but to my surprise, I still remembered it! I preached it again without a note anywhere around. The thought began to take root that maybe I could preach without notes. Then and there, I made a commitment at least to try and see if I could do it.

That time was over 32 years ago. Since then, I have always preached without notes. For seventeen of those years, I was pastor of a church where I preached two different sermons each Sunday. Since 1988, I have been teaching seminary classes in preaching without notes and conducting workshops on it with pastors. Through that time I have developed a systematic approach on learning how to preach without notes. It is one that has been formed through years of struggle, refining, testing. I have listened to others, read the books, learned from students, profited from my own failures and successes with it. I write this book because I feel that what I have learned might be helpful to those who want to preach without notes.

ADVANTAGES

Why would anyone want to preach without notes? There are some positive advantages that come from it.

1. **A direct connection with the people.** Dr. Gordon Clinard, who tried to teach me preaching, once made the statement that preaching was "conversation lifted into the pulpit." That image of preaching as a conversation was a revelation and has been a guiding light for me. When I preach, my hope is to have a personal conversation with another. If five hundred happen to overhear it, well and good. What I want to do is to "converse" with that one and have a dialogue.

Conversations should be direct and personal. They involve face-to-face, eye-to-eye contact. Have you ever talked with someone and through it all, he looked everywhere but at you? He looked over you, to the side, up at the ceiling – anywhere but at you. That gets irritating, doesn't it? I wanted to grab the person's face and say, "Look at me when you are talking to me!"

I can imagine the same sort of feeling can come to the people in the pew listening to us. If we never look at them, establish eye contact with them, it could be a frustrating experience. If we keep bobbing up and down as we look at our notes, we break our connection with them. Maybe they want to shout at us, "If you have got something important to say, look at us when you say it!" I know I have felt that way as I have listened to preachers who are lost in their notes and never seem to want to reach out and involve me in a conversation.

When we are talking with someone, we usually do not have any notes with us. We just share and dialogue with the person. Ideally, this is the way we will preach. Getting rid of notes heightens the possibility that a real conversation about God's truth will take place. Maybe a sign of a good conversation will be someone who says after the service, "I felt you were talking just to me."

2. **It enables us to respond to the people's response.** In any conversation, we are always trying to evaluate how people are responding to what we are saying. Besides their words, there are other indications that give insight into what they are thinking. Facial expressions, eye responses, gestures and body movements – all are clues about how they are hearing us.

In the same manner, the people in the congregation are responding to our sermons. In some traditions, verbal feedback is given and that can let us know how well or how badly we are doing. But even if the response is not verbal, people are responding to what we say. Do we notice their responses? We can see it in their faces and eyes and body actions. However, if we are buried in our notes, it is hard to notice their responses. Good conversation is a dialogue, where we respond to their responses. Preaching without notes frees us to do that.

I noticed many responses when I preached. Sometimes I saw puzzled looks on their faces which meant that I needed to go back and make some idea clearer. Or I saw a nod and a smile which meant that I was on the right wave length with that person. I also saw looks of anger accompanied by unfriendly stares which meant that I had struck a disturbing note. I watched others turn and make comments to another about something I said and I always wondered what it was (maybe I wouldn't want to know). I even saw some yawn, which was not a joy to see, but it meant that I needed to seek to be more interesting.

Freedom from notes enables me to look at people and connect with them. It becomes easier to respond to their response. In delivery, we need to be flexible enough to adapt the sermon to the way the hearers seem to be responding. Without notes, that kind of personal dialogue is easier to accomplish.

3. **It enables us to use our whole selves in the pulpit.** Haddon Robinson, in *Biblical Preaching*[1], referred to a study that determined that seven per cent of a sermon's effectiveness was due to content, and the other 93 per cent was due to body language factors. If this is so, and I feel it is, then we need to pay closer attention to the delivery of the sermon, especially to our body language. Our very physical appearance, facial expressions, gestures, body movements, and the status of our emotions can either help or hinder communication.

When we are tied to notes, it inhibits the freedom we can have in the pulpit. It usually hurts eye contact as we do not look at them, facial expressions are lost because they cannot see them, our gestures become more limited, and our body movement usually stiffens. The total personality does not enter into the preaching moment. The people get half of us, not all of us.

Preaching without notes can free us to bring our whole selves into the pulpit. We can concentrate on having a conversation with another and can give our total selves to it. I have often watched my students carry on conversations in the student center. They were animated, energetic, involved. They gestured, frowned and smiled and questioned, they moved their bodies with meaning. This was what I hoped I would see from them when they preached. Often I did not because they chained themselves to notes that robbed them of their energy and personalities. That was a shame. Preaching without notes can take away those chains and give the freedom to bring the total person into the moment of proclamation.

4. **Most hearers prefer preaching without notes.** Take a survey among your congregation. Ask them which they would prefer: a preacher who uses notes or one who does not. I would guess that they would overwhelmingly prefer the latter. As a church member once said, "I like a preacher who will look me in the eye and shoot straight with the truth." I do, too. The involvement of people in our sermons will rise when we begin to preach without

notes. They might not be able to tell us why, but somehow they know our preaching has gotten better.

Now before some of you hang me out to dry, I know that there are those who preach with notes and do so effectively. Hearers hardly notice that they even have notes. That is great! There is nothing wrong with preaching with notes. But as a general rule, preachers who are good at that are rare. If you use notes, I hope you are working hard to depend less on them. It could be that what I offer in this book might help you leave the notes behind. However, most preachers who use notes could be more effective if they would get rid of them.

The sad state of preaching today has been much discussed and debated. All of us want to improve it. Preaching without notes can help do that. Our people will like it. If done well, interest in our preaching will improve.

5. **It will bring joy to our preaching.** I meet quite a number of ministers who do not particularly like to preach. Standing to speak before a group of people is frightening to them. I relate to that. I have a love/hate relationship with preaching. I love it because I feel it is what God has called me to do. Also, to have the privilege to preach the good news of the gospel is a blessing. But I hate it because it is not easy to do. Maybe I'll forget! Maybe they won't like what I say! Maybe they won't like me! Maybe I will bore them to death! Have such thoughts ever run through your minds? There are times when it seems absurd to think that anybody could preach! Why should we?

We are called to do it, that's why. The message needs to be told and we are the tellers. As I have sought to preach the best I know how and to do so without notes, I have made an amazing discovery! As I work on the preparation of the sermon, the message begins to take control of me, to capture me. It becomes a part of who I am. So when the preaching moment comes, I seem to be "delivering myself." I find great passion and energy for the message. It has become a word that must be spoken. The time of preaching terrifies and humbles me, but I love the chance to do it. I give my total self into preaching and I can do that because I am not chained to a set of notes. I feel a great sense of freedom to preach and it brings to me a great feeling of – joy! That's the word! I find joy in the moment of preaching. That feeling energizes me and I just can not wait to preach again. Somehow the people catch that sense of passion and joy and feel that the time of preaching is a high and holy moment. It becomes a time when the word catches fire and burns again in the hearts of the people.

Do you want that joy in your preaching? It could be that learning the process of preaching without notes can bring it to you. I believe it can! For that reason, I offer to you the suggestions in this book.

OBJECTIONS

There are some difficulties with preaching without notes that need to be faced.

1. **The fear of forgetting.** This is the greatest objection I hear. Preachers are afraid that they will stand to preach and their mind's computer screens will go blank and no key they punch will bring up any ideas. When that happens, they think they will feel ashamed, humiliated, embarrassed. If that happens, I think we are harder on ourselves than our people are. They will understand if we forget and will be eager to forgive. They will encourage us to get ready for next week.

Well, we might forget! That's always a possibility, but I hasten to add, it is not likely. If the preparation that my approach encourages is done seriously, then I feel the chances of forgetting are greatly diminished. You will remember enough. I had a student who preached in class and after a paragraph or two, I knew he was lost. What he was saying did not match the sermon manuscript I had. He had forgotten. But he did not stop. Instead, he remembered enough from his sermon to put something together. The points were rearranged, the illustrations were put in different places, the biblical materials were often given a different slant, but he got through it. The interesting fact was that no one in the class knew he had forgotten anything. To them, what he said had made sense. The student said later that as he preached, he began to remember more and more of the sermon and was able to re-order it to make sense. But no one knew he had forgotten!

14

Some feel that distractions in the congregation could cause them to forget. A child crying, young people talking on the back row, people getting up and leaving, causing you to wonder if you said anything to upset them (probably not). However, when we become as absorbed in the message as I hope my system will help us do, I do not think distractions will veer us off the sermon track.

I think that proper preparation is the key to overcoming the fear of forgetting. The anxiety level about that can be reduced. It involves the courage to risk the possibility that we might forget, but if we do not take the risk, we may never discover that we have the ability to preach without notes. In the years I have taught this subject, only two students out of seventy forgot parts of their sermons, and one of those successfully preached without notes later. It is worth taking the risk to see what might happen.

2. **The fear that we might forget to say something important.** Again, not likely. If we have prepared well, we should surely remember the important points. Usually if we forget something, it is not all that important anyway. If it is, remember this. We still have 51 more Sundays in the year to say it.

3. **The temptation to become lazy.** I have a fear about this. Some feel that learning to preach without notes will save a lot of preparation time. In the long run, it might. However, to preach without notes may take more time to prepare, not less. If you want an easier way to prepare to preach, my approach will not be it. But if you want to see if your preaching can become more effective, the price you pay to learn this method will be worth it. If preaching is a priority to us, we will be willing to give the extra effort needed to do it.

Also, preaching without notes is not learning to preach "off the cuff." One of the dangers as preachers is that we talk so much we can fall into the belief that we can always summon up an appropriate word in an instant, "off the cuff." Don't fall into that trap! Sermons need to be prepared thoroughly. We must think through what we need to say before we say it. Preaching without notes involves serious preparation. It will not be for the lazy.

A CHALLENGE

If you have read this far, I assume you are interested in learning how to preach without notes. I invite you to take a journey through the process I have developed. Give it a try! See if it might work for you!

I know that not all preachers can preach without notes, nor should they. Each person must find the method of delivery that is most comfortable. You may not end up preaching without notes. Even so, I believe that studying the method I present has the possibility of improving your preaching, even though you will still use notes.

Maybe somebody will say to you soon, "You preachers ought to preach without notes." Your reaction? "I could never do that!" Are you sure? More can do it than think they can. Will you have the courage to risk finding out? The only way you will know if you can – or can not – is to try. I challenge you to try.

---

1. Haddon W. Robinson, *Biblical Preaching* (Grand Rapids: Baker Book House, 1980), 193.

Chapter Two

Toward Simplicity: Finding The Right Road Map

After reading and listening to hundreds, yea thousands, of sermons, I am convinced that their greatest weakness is a lack of focus. They often go everywhere, leading to confusion and bewilderment. A pastor, having listened to such a rambling sermon, made the judgment, "When he got up to preach, he didn't know where he was going and when he sat down, he didn't know where he'd been."

I have heard and preached many sermons like that. Often in conducting workshops, I ask the pastors a "trick" question. "How many points did your sermon have Sunday?" They quickly reply, "two" or "three" or "four." After they answer, I tell them that they had one or two or three more points in their sermon than they needed. I then emphasize that sermons should have only *one* point. That point may be developed in two or three or four ways, but one point is all that a sermon seeks to communicate. Finding that one idea is often the hardest work in preparing to preach. But limiting it to one idea may be just as hard. If we do not limit it to one good idea, then our sermons are usually out of focus. It is like a TV picture that is blurred, or has snow, or has static on it. We will fiddle with the controls until we can get it into as sharp a focus as we can. That is what we need to do with our sermons, especially if we want to preach without notes.

I compare the development of a sermon to finding the right road map for a trip. If I want to go from Sioux Falls, South Dakota to Richmond, Virginia, I will not plan to go via Denver, Dallas, or New Orleans. Instead, I will seek to find the simplest, straightest, most direct route possible. I want to find the main interstates and

17

travel on them, avoiding side roads and detours that might get me lost.

To preach without notes, we need to develop the simplest road map for our sermonic journeys. We want the simplest, clearest, most direct route possible. We must stay off the side roads that could confuse us and get us lost. A pastor friend dropped by the office to ask me honestly to evaluate some sermons I had heard him preach. I told him that they seemed "scattered," that I could not discern where he was going with them. He replied, "You mean I ought to take seriously all those ideas I learned in seminary about thesis and objective?" Bingo! We professors teach those concepts for a reason. They will help us get a clearly focused sermon.

So the first crucial step in preaching without notes is to develop the simplest road map possible of the sermon, so clearly focused that it will be easy to remember. In this chapter, I want to review some of the important concepts we learned in Preaching 101. It might seem like "old hat" to us, but we need to be sure of our terms and approaches.

Now I am making an assumption as we begin. I assume that you have honestly wrestled with the biblical truth found in the text. We seek to present sermons whose content and form are true to the scripture. We are committed to being faithful biblical preachers. A lot of books are available to help us understand how to preach biblically.[1] Before a sermon can be created, the biblical study must be done.

Having done the serious Bible study, where do we travel from there?

BASIC ROUTE: CENTRAL IDEA OF THE TEXT

The Bible was written in a specific time, to specific people, for a specific purpose, in a specific language, by specific persons. One of our tasks is to try as best we can to understand what the biblical word was *then*. All the brainstorming of ideas, all the work with commentaries and word studies, all the language and theological discussions, are for the purpose of helping us discover the central idea of the text we are considering. In that place and time, what was the Word of the Lord? This is the foundational biblical truth that we want to communicate. I feel it is like the basic route on our sermon journey. We want to get from Sioux Falls to Richmond, that is our hope. In a sermon, it is our hope to help people understand and apply the basic biblical truth in the text.

At this point, the emphasis is on the "then," the historical past. After all the study we do, what do we think is the one – main idea – that our scripture presents? Can we state it in a brief sentence? I encourage my students to strive to state the central idea of the text (CIT) in a brief sentence, in the past tense, with the freedom to use historical references and names. But that sentence must *not* have any "ands" in it. Sentences with "ands" usually present more than one idea. Until they can come up with such a sentence, they are not ready to develop a sermon.

Throughout this chapter, I will seek to illustrate the homiletical principles from three different texts. I hope they will help to clarify the ideas presented.

1.   I Samuel 17:28-51. This is the familiar story of David and Goliath. What would a good and bad CIT look like?

   GOOD: With God's help, David killed Goliath.

   BAD: With God's help and with his slingshot, David killed Goliath. This is bad because it presents two ideas — God's help and David's slingshot. The text puts the basic emphasis on David's trust in God to help him defeat Goliath. We should stick to that main idea and organize the sermon around it.

2.   Micah 6:8. This text is the answer to, "What does the Lord require of us?"

   GOOD: Micah called the people to righteous living.

   BAD: Micah called the people to do justice, love kindness, and walk humbly with God. This sentence contains the points of the sermon. The CIT should be the summation of what the points say. Do not include the points of a sermon in the CIT (or thesis).

3.   Luke 15:11-24 This is the story of the "prodigal son."

   GOOD: The father welcomed the prodigal son back home.

   BAD: The father welcomed the prodigal son back home

and his older brother got mad. Two ideas here. Emphasize only one of them.

The CIT is a starting point for developing a good road map of the sermon. In a sentence, what do we think the text said? We need to get that idea finely tuned, sharply focused.

INTERSTATE: THE THESIS

With the overall driving route in mind, it is time to get practical. Exactly which roads will get me where I want to go? It is time to choose the interstate to travel. It will be the road that actually gets me on the way.

Such is the thesis. It has been called by many terms – proposition, focus statement, main thought. It is the one idea we are going to preach, the sermon summed up in a sentence. If our people take one truth from our sermon, hopefully it will be this one. It is the practical truth for living today. It is what the sermon text means now. It is the contemporary truth.

We must bring the biblical truth into the now. Renowned preacher Harry Emerson Fosdick made the comment that preachers must not live with the expectation that people come to church anxiously wanting to know what the Jebusites did 10,000 years ago.[2] Who cares? I know I don't! What I am interested in is how what the Jebusites did so long ago makes a difference in my life now. This is what our sermons should help others see.

Students complain that it is hard to get a thesis sentence. (I always tell them if they ever hear me say that anything about preaching is easy, it is time to put me out to pasture). However, we must do it. If we are not clear about what we want to say, it will not be clear to our people.

But here is a bonus! If we have worked hard to get a good CIT in a sentence, stating the thesis will not be so hard. All we need to do is to take the CIT and contemporize it by putting it into the present tense, and then personalize it by using personal pronouns. To "contemporize" and "personalize" helps the biblical truth of yesterday become a biblical truth for today. Let's see how it works.

David

CIT: With God's help, David killed Goliath.

Thesis: With God's help, we (personalize) can kill (contemporize) our (personalize) giants.

Micah

CIT: Micah called the people to righteous living.

Thesis: We (personalize) are to live (contemporize) righteously.

Prodigal Son

CIT: The father welcomed the prodigal son back home.

Thesis: The Father welcomes (contemporize) us (personalize) prodigals back home.

In the thesis, do not include "ands," historical names or places, or the points of the sermon. Keep it contemporary and personal.

To preach without notes, we must be very clear about our sermon idea. We should know this idea "by heart." As we develop our sermon, any idea that does not relate to this thesis must be eliminated. That will help keep the sermon focused and easier to remember. What are you going to preach about this Sunday? Can you tell me in a sentence?

THE CITY: GENERAL OBJECTIVE

Imagine asking people where they were going on their trip and they said, "We have no idea. We're just going to start out and see where it takes us." We might think that strange! It reminds us of the old adage that if you don't know where you're going, you're probably going to get there. Have you ever heard sermons like that? The preacher starts out and lets the sermon go where it will. Most of the time, it never seems to arrive anywhere. It just goes here and there.

Focused trips have destinations. So do focused sermons. There is a beginning and an ending. Before we get on the road, we plan on where we will get off it. The trip has purpose, destination.

To preach without notes, we need to have a clear picture of our destination. Where are we going with the sermon? What do we hope happens because of it? What is the objective? One such objective is what I call the general or major objective. If I set out for my mother's house, my general objective is the city where she lives, Petersburg, Virginia. I must get there before I can find her house. Likewise, a sermon seeks to deal with general areas of the Christian life. It needs to focus on one of these general areas. (A sermon will get more specific in these general areas, but that is coming later.) In seminary, I learned to focus in on six general areas. Through the years, they have served me well.

1. **Evangelistic.** The general area is evangelism with the hope that others will find Christ through the sermon. The sermon is directed to this goal. Anything that does not help to accomplish it is material for another sermon.

2. **Supportive.** The general area is comfort and the hope is that the sermon will provide others with support for the hard times of their lives.

3. **Doctrinal/Teaching.** The general area is learning and the hope is that the sermon will teach them important information they need to know.

4. **Devotional.** The general area is one's personal relationship with God and the hope of the sermon is that they will deepen their love for God. Sermons on prayer, meditation, and worship fall into this category.

5. **Ethical.** The general area is the Christian's relationship to others and to the environment. The sermon's hope is to encourage proper Christian ethical actions. Sermons on euthanasia, war, ecology, etc., are included here.

6. **Consecrational.** The general area is Christian discipleship and the hope is to develop a deeper commitment to Christ. This is by far the largest category for sermons. Subjects such as love, stewardship, witnessing, growth, etc., are included.

A sermon needs to be focused into one area – and one area only! Now understand! These areas will overlap. A sermon directed to one general area may touch another, or may touch them all. For example, an evangelistic sermon can also provide support for people as they remember their salvation; it can teach them as they learn the way of salvation; it can draw them closer to God as they remember how much they are loved; it can lead them to treat others with greater respect ethically as they see them as loved by God;

and it can cause them to become better disciples as they commit themselves to witnessing to the good news.

While this may happen and usually does, zero in on one area only. We need to shape our sermons to fit one general destination. Focus it sharply on that. Let the Holy Spirit apply the sermon as needed! To preach without notes, we must focus in on one general objective.

THE HOUSE: SPECIFIC OBJECTIVE

Once I get to Petersburg, my next destination is more specific, 1842 East Boulevard. When I get there, I get out of the car, go into the house, hug my mother, sit down and celebrate the fact that I have arrived. The trip is over. I got where I wanted to go.

A sermon should do that. It should arrive at a specific destination. It gets into the specific "houses" of the people. The question to ask is this: If the people do what the sermon challenges them to do, what one action will it be? After all is said and done, what do we hope happens because of the sermon? For sermons are not just holy "chit-chats." They seek to persuade. What one action do we want to persuade them to do in the sermon?

In my judgment, if we have a good thesis statement, a specific objective (SO) will not be hard to determine. All we need to do is to put the thesis "into action." The SO is the action statement of the thesis. As a simple technique, I suggest that we start the SO with the words, "that they will...." This focuses in on the action. Let's take a look at the sermon examples.

Thesis: With God's help, we can kill our giants.
SO: That they will, with God's help, kill their giants.
Thesis: We are to live righteously.
SO: That they will live righteously.
Thesis: The Father welcomes us prodigals back home.
SO: That they will let the Father welcome them back home.

The SO is the "thesis with legs." It is getting out of the car, walking into the house, and sitting down. What we planned has come to pass. We have arrived!

If we relate the SO to the general objectives, it would look like this:

General Objective	Specific Objective
Evangelistic	That they will trust Christ.
Supportive	That they will be comforted.
Teaching	That they will learn some truth.
Devotional	That they will draw closer to God.
Ethical	That they will live ethical lives.
Consecrational	That they will be better disciples.

The SO is why we preach the sermon. It is the truth we hope will happen among the people. To preach without notes, this destination must always be clear in our minds. Any material that does not help us accomplish the SO is not for the sermon. We must focus, focus, focus!

TRIP NAME: THE TITLE

Almost without thinking, we usually give names to the big trips we take. We refer to the "trip home" or "the family reunion trip" or "the trip to Florida." When we refer to those names, everyone knows which trip we are talking about.

Likewise, sermons need names. We call that name a "title." Unfortunately, the importance of titles has often been downplayed in sermon preparation. I regret that. A good title not only hints at what the sermon is about, but it also serves as another guidepost for focusing the sermon. A proper title sets the boundary lines for the sermon. There is always a key word in a title that designates the direction the sermon will go. To go outside the confines of that word is to step "out of bounds." For example, the title, "The Questions of Prayer," means that the sermon is going to be about the questions surrounding prayer, not the postures for prayer, or the language of prayer, or specific answers to prayer. Only material that deals with the questions on prayer should be included in the sermon. Everything else is off limits.

As I see it, there are six general types of sermon titles. Each of them has a key word. Using our sermon examples, how might the sermon titles be charted?

Type	Key Word	Sermon Titles
Emphatic	Strong Noun	"The **Way** to Victory"
		"The **Call** for Living"
		"The **Forgiveness** of God"
Limiting Word	Descriptive Word	"The Way to **Overwhelming** Victory"
		"The Call to **Righteous** Living"
		"The **Forgiving** Love of God"
Verbal	Verb	"Victory **Comes** From God"
		"Righteousness **Is** Living!"
		"**Going** Home"
Imperative	Imperative	"**Fight** the Giants!"
		"**Live** Righteously!"
		"**Seek** Forgiveness!"
Question	Interrogative	"**How** Do We Face Giants?"
		"**What** Does God Require?"
		"**Is** There a Way Home?"
Poetic	Metaphor	"On Killing Giants"
		"The Right Life-Style"
		"A Welcome Home"

The Poetic type is a creative approach to titles. It relies heavily upon the use of metaphor to capture the essence of the sermon. The sermon content will establish the meaning of the creative title.

A good title keeps us on the right interstate. It will not let us get off at the wrong ramp. It will help us encapsule the sermon in our minds. That will be a valuable aid to preaching without notes.

SIGNPOSTS: SERMON DEVELOPMENT

When I map out my trip from Sioux Falls to my mother's house in Virginia, I note several mini-destinations along the way. I must go through Kansas City, St. Louis, Louisville, Richmond, and then home. These cities become significant signposts on the trip, letting me know that I am making progress and am headed in the right direction.

A sermon needs such signposts along the way. They have been called points, steps, moves, divisions. These are the distinctive blocks of thought that help us develop our sermon and accomplish our thesis and objective. It is how we plot our sermon. Such signposts help us to keep the sermon moving in the right direction.

There are many ways to develop a sermon. Variety is the spice of sermon making. I have dealt with possible approaches elsewhere.[3] However, it does seem that there are two major ways to develop a sermon.

1. **Deductive approach.** The old saying in preaching was that you "tell them what you are going to say, you say it, then you tell them what you said." That is the deductive approach. It does three things:

A. It starts with the biblical truth and then moves to the needs of the people.

B. It states the thesis in the sermon introduction and the points then "prove" that truth. The flow is from a general idea to specific applications.

C. It has a logical approach, with a linear development of the idea.

Many have called this the "three points and a poem" approach and have discarded it, feeling it has outlived its usefulness. But that is not necessarily so. There are times when the best approach to a sermon may be deductive. Having a deductive outline does not "kill" a sermon. Other factors, such as content, relevancy, and delivery contribute to its worth – or lack of it.

Looking at two of our sermon examples, what would a deductive outline look like? Thesis: With God's help, we can kill our giants. How?

I. God gives us courage for the fight – he did not fear the giant

II. God gives us gifts for the fight – David's sling, not Saul's armor

III. God gives us strength for the fight – "The Lord will deliver you into my hand"

From Micah 6:8. Thesis: We are to live righteously. How?

I. We will do justice.

II. We will love kindness.

III. We will walk humbly with God.

We must strive for the simple and clear outline, one that will be easy to follow and remember.

2. **Inductive Approach.** This approach has been emphasized a great deal in recent homiletic circles. There are three facets of it.

A. The sermon starts with the experience of the people and then moves them to scripture. It starts where they are and "connects" their situation to the text.

B. It states the thesis in the conclusion. The sermon takes the people on a search for truth that will not be completed until the end of the sermon.

C. It moves from a specific action to a general truth.

There is no doubt that this is an inviting way to preach a sermon. Narrative material especially fits this mold. For example, a sermon on the prodigal son might be plotted this way:

Step 1: We are selfish. "Give me what I want"

Step 2: We waste it all. "Riotous living"

Step 3: We fall to the bottom. "Pig sty"

Step 4: We repent. "Better to be a servant in my Father's house."

Step 5: Thesis: Our Father welcomes us prodigals back home. "My son was lost, now is found"

In my view, the difference between a deductive/inductive approach is similar to the different approaches to a murder mystery. In the deductive mode, we know who the killer is right from the start and the rest of the show awaits the discovery of what we know by the characters. At the end, we say, "Finally, they figured it out!" In an inductive approach, we do not know who the murderer is and, throughout the show, we try to figure it out along with the characters. When we find out who it is at the end, we either say joyfully, "I was right," or sadly, "I was wrong." Which mystery approach do you like? If well done, both of them can work successfully.

There are many other types of sermon "outlines," such as order of time, theses/antithesis/synthesis, problem/solution, chase outline, cause/effect, etc. Many books are available to help us develop our sermons.[4] The important point is that to preach without notes we must know where we are going and how we are going to get there. What are the significant signposts in our sermon? Hopefully, they are arranged in such a way that Point A leads to Point B, and Point B leads to Point C, and so on. It has a smooth, natural flow. We must know the signposts like the back of our hands. They will help us remember the sermon.

THE FINAL MAP: THE COVER PAGE

I have reviewed all the basic homiletical ideas for a purpose. The hope is that we can develop a summation of our sermon plan, an overall final map of the journey the sermon will take. I feel we must do that if we are to preach without notes. I call this summation a "cover page." It deals with the essential matters of the sermon. It will be a good guide to the sermon route.

COVER PAGE

Text

Title

CIT – Biblical truth, past tense

Thesis – present tense, contemporary, personal

GO – **One** of the 6 major areas of Christian living

SO – The thesis in action: "That they will…"

Body – The significant signposts of the sermon development

With this in mind, the cover pages of our sermon examples would finally take these forms:

1. Text: 1 Samuel 17:28-51
   Title: When Goliaths Arise
   CIT: With God's help, David killed Goliath.
   Thesis: With God's help, we can kill our giants.
   GO: Consecrational
   SO: That they will depend on God's help to kill their giants.

Body Signposts:

Problem: Giants that terrify us.

Solution: God will help us defeat the giants.

2. Text: Micah 6:8

   Title: The Requirements We Have

   CIT: Micah called the people to live righteously.

   Thesis: We are to live righteously.

   GO: Consecrational

   SO: That they will live righteously.

   Body Signposts:

       I. We will do justice.

       II. We will love kindness.

       III. We will walk humbly with God.

3. Text: Luke 15:11-24

   Title: If We Go Back Home

   CIT: The father welcomed the prodigal son back home.

   Thesis: The Father will welcome us prodigals back home.

   GO: Supportive

   SO: That they will find God's forgiveness "back home."

   Body Signposts:

       I. We rebel

       II. We suffer

       III. We repent

       IV. We find forgiveness from God

Developing – and learning – such a cover page is an essential step in learning how to preach without notes. It focuses our sermon and serves as the overarching framework for it. This cover page information is like the final road map that we determine will help us take our journey. It is the basic road plan. The cover page is the basic road map for our sermon journey. If we memorize anything (and I do not stress outright memorization in my system), let us memorize the cover page. Honestly, I do not think remembering it will be too much of a problem. As hard as we have worked to get our idea and objective and sermon signposts, how can we forget them? The week before we preach, those items get into our "blood stream" and become a part of us. We can not forget them! When that happens, we are on our way to preaching without notes.

Through it all, we must strive for simplicity. To preach without notes, there are some things we cannot do. We must avoid complex ideas, complex sermon development, long, involved arguments. The old cliches are true. "Less is more!" and "The simpler, the better!" Such simplicity will help us remember the sermon more easily.

So we have a simple road map for the journey. Now we must decide what we need to take with us to help us make the trip. What do we need to pack? How much gas do we need? Where will we get food? How long will the trip take? Who will do the driving? All of these matters are the "nuts and bolts" components of a trip. If we are to take the trip successfully, we need to decide about them.

A sermon has "nuts and bolts" components also. They are such matters as what material to use, which illustrations are the best, how long will the sermon be, what applications should be made, what words will be used. In order for our sermonic journeys to be successful, we must answer these questions. And for us, there is another question to consider. How can we do it all so that we can finally preach the sermon without notes? To these matters, we now turn.

---

1. See Ronald J. Allen, *Contemporary Biblical Interpretation for Preaching* (Valley Forge: Judson Press, 1984); Charles Bugg, *Preaching From the Inside Out* (Nashville: Broadman Press, 1992); James Cox, *Preaching* (San Francisco: Harper and Row, 1985); Wayne McDill, *The 12 Essential Skills for Great Preaching* (Nashville: Broadman Press, 1994); Clyde Fant, *Preaching for Today* (San Francisco: Harper, 1987); Al Fasol, *Essentials for Biblical Preaching* (Grand Rapids: Baker Book House, 1989); Haddon W. Robinson, *Biblical Preaching* (Grand Rapids: Baker Book House, 1980).

2. Harry Emerson Fosdick, *The Living of These Days* (New York: Harper, 1950), 92.

3. See Hugh Litchfield, "Outlining the Sermon", *Handbook of Contemporary Preaching*, Michael Duduit, ed. (Nashville: Broadman Press, 1992), 162-174.

4. See Fred Craddock, *Preaching* (Nashville: Abingdon Press, 1988); Milton Crum, Jr., *Manual on Preaching* (Valley Forge: Judson Press, 1977); Grady Davis, *Design for Preaching* (Philadelphia: Muhlenberg Press, 1958); Harold Freeman, *Variety in Biblical Preaching* (Waco, Texas: Word Books, 1987); Ralph Lewis with Greg Lewis, *Inductive Preaching* (Westchester, Illinois: Crossway Books, 1976); Eugene Lowry, *The Homiletical Plot* (Atlanta: John Knox Press, 1980); James Earl Massey, *Designing the Sermon* (Nashville: Abingdon Press, 1980); Don Wardlaw, ed., *Preaching Biblically* (Philadelphia: Westminster Press, 1983).

Chapter Three

Developing Pictures:
The Ability To See

When my children were small, often they would see something that excited them and would come and try to tell me what they had seen. But their vocabulary was not well developed yet, and so they had trouble putting it into words. Sometimes I would give them a piece of paper and ask them to draw a picture of what they had seen. That they could do. They could make a picture of it, even though they could not describe it well in words.

However, in our sermons we need to construct clear word pictures of the images we see. We usually can not take a piece of paper and draw literal pictures for the people, so we must provide the best "language pictures" that we can. In a true sense, we preachers are artists, but we paint our pictures in words. Through them, we can help others "see" the truth we seek to preach.

Before we can do that, we must develop the pictures in our own mind. Can we think in pictures? Can we see in our imaginations the truths we want to present? To preach without notes, this becomes a very key issue. We need to work to develop our sermons into pictures, pictures that follow one another in a logical, smooth pattern. Pictures and images become the building blocks for our sermonic journey. I have discovered that, having gone from Sioux Falls to Richmond before, when I think about taking the trip now, I put it into pictures and images. I imagine the grain mill in Iowa, Arrowhead Stadium in Kansas City, the Arch in St. Louis, the Cracker Barrel Restaurant in Kentucky, the West Virginia Turnpike, the Texaco station in the Virginia mountains. These are the places I will pass on the way home. So when I imagine the trip, I do not see it in just cold road numbers and city names, but in pictures that remind me of people and places and feelings and smells. Somehow, in thinking that way about the trip, it does not seem as hard to drive anymore.

What I hope to do with a sermon is to picture it in such a fashion. I do not want to see the sermon as just words to be said, but pictures to be described. Just as I wanted my children to tell me what they had seen, I feel a sermon needs to tell the people what we see as we wrestle with the truth. The ultimate goal is to put the sermon together like a movie, scene after scene, action shot after action shot. In that way, a sermon will come alive and be a living word. It will not be just outlines and definitions, but images and pictures that help the hearers to feel and see and experience the truth.

As we prepare our sermons, what pictures come to mind? Can we see the sermon in action? In preaching without notes, we will seek to put the sermon together through stories and images. This chapter will deal with the issue of "seeing" the stories and pictures. In the next chapter, the more specific development of images and image outlines will be discussed.

THE BIBLICAL MATERIAL IN PICTURES

Recently I went to see the movie *Gettysburg*, the four-hour re-creation of that famous battle of the Civil War. I have always been a Civil War "buff" and through the years read a lot of books on Gettysburg. I went there and toured the battlefields. I studied pictures about it and saw models that depicted all the battles of that three-day engagement. After all that reading and studying, in my mind I imagined a picture of how the battle must have been fought. In a way, through such pictures, I became a spectator to it, watching as the soldiers marched bravely into battle, overhearing the generals plot their battle plans, looking on as the Confederate soldiers made that futile charge against the firmly entrenched Union line in the pivotal encounter known as Pickett's Charge. Then I saw the movie and learned how others viewed the battle. Many of my imagined pictures were the same as in the movie, many were not. But it was exciting to see the movie, to watch as the pictures I had imagined came to life. History seemed like a present event and it felt like I was there.

34

In the same way, I hope we can use our imaginations to picture the biblical texts we preach. Hopefully, when we wrestled with the text to try to understand it, pictures were being formed in our minds concerning the text. Can we imagine the text coming to life, the characters actually breathing and acting, the events happening again, the words really being said? Now I know that is not easy to do and that we can never "reconstruct" the historical context perfectly. Even so, I feel we can picture it well enough to get the sense and feel of it. We need to examine well the text so that we might become "spectators" to it, standing on the fringes of the action, watching it unfold. Through our imaginations, we can see Cain kill Abel, or hear David's cry of repentance, watch as Paul writes a letter to the Philippians from that prison cell, feel the joy of the disciples as they go out shouting, "He is alive!" Can we imagine ourselves in those scenes and movements? Do the texts come alive for us?

For a long time, we have tried to imagine the Bible coming to life. We have sought to do that through drama. Once I preached a sermon series on some of the parables and to help them come alive, some of the church members presented mini-dramas of them. The performers dressed up in the ancient costumes and sought to re-create the action and dialogue of the parable. Over and over again, I heard the reaction, "I understand the parable better now. I can really see it." "For the first time, the parable came alive for me." Such is our hope in dealing with the Bible. So we put on Christmas plays and Easter pageants so that these great events might come alive to others. By doing that, they can "see" the biblical events and imagine themselves there.

In our imaginations, we need to re-create the biblical scenes as best we can. If we can see them happening in our minds, then what we do as we preach is describe what we see to the people. In my life, others are always coming up to me and saying, "Let me tell you what I saw!" With excitement, animation, and involvement, they do. And they do not have note one in their hands! They did not need them. They just described what they had seen. In preaching without notes, when we deal with the biblical material, ideally we see the ideas alive in pictures and all we have to do is to tell the people what we see – excitedly, with animation, deeply involved. We will not need notes to do that.

So we watch as David approaches that fierce, gigantic, terror of a man called Goliath. Can we imagine the taunting of Goliath, the fear on the faces of the Israelites looking on, the calm assurance of David as he begins to twirl his slingshot? Can we hear the sound of the rock hitting Goliath, watch in shock as he staggers, feel the ground shake as his huge body comes crashing to the earth? Can we see the soldiers standing there stunned as David cuts off Goliath's head? Can we hear the screams and cries of joy when the Israelites realize that victory is theirs? What a scene! How can we not picture that? Can we not put ourselves into that scene?

Or let us overhear as Micah preaches to his people. They want to know why God has not made life better for them. They want to judge and question God. But Micah reminds them that they are the ones on the witness stand and God is questioning them. Then we listen as Micah makes that chilling statement. "What does God require of you?" How can they please God? "Here it is," Micah says. "Do justice, love kindness, and walk humbly with God." What do they think of that? Will they do it?

Or surely we can see that beaten young boy walking back home from that pig sty. Can you visualize the look of fear and doubt on his face? What will his father say – or do? Will he reject him, laugh at him, ignore him? Then can we not see the father going out again to take that long look down the road, a look that he had taken so many times before? But this time, he sees someone in the distance! He strains to get a better look. Then he recognizes his son, and off he runs – not walks – but runs to met the startled boy, throws his arms around him and celebrates. "My son was dead, but he is alive." How can we not see that, be moved by that? Can we not preach that with passion and involvement?

Now the objection may come that it is easier to do that with some biblical material than it is with others. There is no doubt about that. Some texts seem hard to picture. Even so, I feel we can still picture most biblical texts.

The easiest material to picture are the **historical stories**, **narrative material** and **the Gospels**. They usually have a well-defined plot, good action, colorful characters. Much of the Bible is couched in this kind of literary genre. As we work with such texts let them take flesh and blood and come alive in our imaginations. Let us "step" into the scenes and see and hear and feel them happening.

Poetry is prominent in the Bible. Poetry is the language of the feelings and is written in metaphors and similes and word pictures. Images pop out at us in poetry. So the Lord is pictured as a shepherd caring for the sheep (Ps. 23), as a refuge or fortress in our time of need (Ps. 46), as our rock of salvation (Ps. 62). Our search for God is likened to a deer longing for water to quench its thirst (Ps. 42), the faithfulness of God as One who is inclined and straining toward us (Ps. 17), and the love of God is pictured as a deliverer who will come to save us in our time of trouble (Ps. 54). Pictures and images abound in the Psalms and in the poetic language of the Bible. Such is the language of the poet. Can we feel it, sense the differing moods, describe the struggles and triumphs there? We need to picture these images and metaphors and describe them to others.

The **Prophets** are full of material that can be imaged. Each prophet dealt with a certain issue and a particular time. Their language is full of metaphors and images. Jeremiah buys a plot of land, even though the area will soon be captured by the enemy, a sign of his hope in God's sovereignty. Hosea goes and buys rebellious Gomer out of her slavery, a sign of the love God has for the rebellious people of Israel. Jonah preaches a great revival in Ninevah and then sits on top of a hill, upset about the inclusiveness of the love of God. Habakkuk stands in a watchtower, wondering if there is hope coming from God, but believing that in due time, God's victory would come and the people would be saved. Nehemiah rebuilds the wall of Jerusalem against tremendous odds, a sign that God's blessing was still with the people. We cannot read the prophets without getting caught up in the drama. To me, it seems easy to "step" into their moments, see the terrible sins of the time, hear the words of warning and hope that the prophets speak. The pictures are there for the seeing.

Wisdom literature is tougher to picture, but not impossible. **Proverbs** is full of short sayings that illustrate wisdom. These sayings are picturesque, pointing to vivid images. We need to picture the images that the proverbs describe. For example, can we picture the two different kinds of people mentioned in Proverbs 13:1? "A wise son hears his father's instruction, but a scoffer does not listen to rebuke." Have we ever known such people? Have we ever been like that? Is not this proverb true to life? Or in 24:13, wisdom is likened to honey, "sweet to your taste." I can almost taste the flavor of that sweet liquid. What a word picture! Proverbs present the truth in these kinds of visual images. We can picture how the proverbs "live" in everyday life. See them in action.

Ecclesiastes is a story of a person on a search for the good life. He tries everything he can think of, but he is not satisfied. Again, the story is told in some beautiful images and word pictures. For example, in talking about our need of each other, the writer gives some quick pictures in 4:9-12. "Two are better than one, because they have a good reward for their toil (two workers can do more than one). For if they fall, one will lift up his fellow; but woe to him who is alone when he falls and has not another to lift him up (two can encourage each other in the hard times). Again, if two lie together they are warm, but how can one be warm alone (two can help meet each other's needs)? And though a man might prevail against one who is alone, two will withstand him. A threefold cord is not quickly broken (two can protect each other against evil)." Ecclesiastes has a lot of these kinds of quick, picturesque images. It is a good source for our imaginations. Can we picture the power of friendship, of being together? The images are so true to life.

The Song of Solomon, however we interpret it, is full of word pictures and images that are not hard to imagine. There are some magnificent pictures of the beauty of love. **Job** is a drama full of tension, plot, and a cast of very colorful characters. God and the devil talking, the terrible devastation, friends who do not really comfort Job, Job crying out against God, and then God coming to speak to Job through the whirlwind. Our imaginations should not find it hard to step into this story and picture it.

When we come to the **Letters** of the New Testament, the task of picturing the ideas seems more difficult. But again, it is not impossible. To begin with, the letters have historical contexts, written to specific people for specific purposes. We need to picture our way into these contexts. So, as best as I understand it, Romans was written to the Church in Rome that Paul was hoping to visit. Through that letter, Paul let them know the basics of his theology. The Corinthian writings are a series of letters passed back and forth between Paul and the church, dealing with very specific problems. Philippians was written from a jail cell, a thank-you note by Paul to the church for the gift brought to him by Epaphroditus. Philemon was written to encourage that Christian man to welcome back Onesimus, the run-away slave, as a brother in Christ. The letters of John were written to deal with a prominent person who was causing quite a problem in the church. And so it goes! Through our study of the texts, we should be able to understand the contexts of those letters and seek to "see" them as they were written, to step into their scenes.

What about the language of the letters? It is often prose language, heavy with theological words and concepts and definitions. This is where word studies enter into the picture. When we study the meaning of the major words in the text, what we usually get are – pictures! For here is a truth I trust. Before there were words, there were pictures. People saw a funny animal flying in the sky first, and only later did they call it by the word "bird." The symbol or picture was first. In preaching, we need to get beyond the words to the pictures or images they describe. So the word "sin" can be pictured as an archer shooting an arrow that misses the center of the target. So "love" is described as Jesus climbing a cross and sacrificing his life for the world. So "justification" can be seen as a court scene, where we are judged guilty by God. But Christ intercedes on our behalf, saying, "I died for them," and then hearing a new verdict, "forgiven!" "Law" is seen as a prison that takes away our freedom, while "grace" is the key that opens the door and sets us free. What are the pictures behind the words? What scenes are taking place? What images are provoked by the words? Through a serious study of the text, I believe we can find the word pictures needed upon which we can hang our sermons.

Apocalyptic language, in books such as Revelation and Daniel, is characterized by its dramatic imagery. The imagination seems

39

to run wild in this genre. We should be able to picture it more easily than some language types. Some of the pictures we get might look weird, but they will be very "eye-catching." The drama of the apocalyptic books is fun to depict. See the action, feel the tension and moods, celebrate the victory! In preaching, we describe the pictures we see.

To preach without notes, we need to labor to get the truth into pictures, and then we describe the pictures to others. When studying the basic idea of the text, keep in mind this thought. When I describe this idea, it will look "like this." What does the truth "look" like? I feel this is a key to preaching effectively and definitely a key to preaching without notes. Salvation is like – what? Hope is like – what? What pictures do the words point us to? We must find them, and then describe them to our people.

One of the benefits of television is its ability to take us all over the world. If something happens in Africa, or England, or in the town 50 miles down the road, television takes us there and shows it to us. We see the places, the people, the events. In the same manner, our sermons need verbally to take people to the biblical scenes, enabling them to see the characters, hear the noises, see the landscape, feel the tension. It is a monumental challenge! But we must struggle to do it. It will help the truth come alive. We must do everything we can to treat the text honestly, respectfully. Then we must do everything we can to picture it in the best way possible.

One exercise I do with students is to have them stand in the pulpit and I will then ask them to tell me a certain biblical story. They have no notes, have not prepared what they will say, but the story is familiar to them. I want them to tell me the story as it comes to their minds, and tell it in such a way that I will be drawn into the story. They usually stumble a bit at first, but then they relax and get into it. What they need to do is to trust their knowledge of the story and their ability to tell it. Through this exercise, they usually begin to gain confidence in themselves to tell the story without the use of notes. I also sometimes give them a word, like salvation, and ask them to describe that concept to me in a picture. What image comes to mind? They usually come up with some kind of picture. I can see the excitement on their faces as they realize that they can imagine some picture that captures the essence of the idea. These are exercises you might try in the privacy of the sanctuary. Can you see and tell the biblical stories? If so, you are learning how to preach without notes.

THE APPLICATION AS PICTURE

Part of the sermon will involve picturing the meaning of the biblical text. Another part will be to apply this meaning to the people now. The truth of scripture must take flesh and blood and walk among the lives of those to whom we preach. Our sermons will hopefully be used by the Spirit to make a difference in their lives. We must place the truth in their laps and see what they do with it.

Sermons are meant to be "people specific." Too many sermons seek to preach to "Christians in general." They say, "Christians need to love one another," or "Christians need to battle the evils of racism," or "Christians need to witness more." No, it is not "Christians." *We* need to love more, *we* need to battle racism, *we* need to witness more. We do not preach to Christians in general, we preach to Mary and Tom and George and Beth, and they are right there in the pews in front of us. The sermon is for them. We need to get into their "kitchens" with the food of truth. Sermons are to make a difference in their lives. When we prepare our sermons, we must speak to their context.

Many have told me that they have great difficulty in applying the sermon to today. They can understand the biblical idea, but bringing it across the thousands of years to today is confusing. How can what happened then matter now? The biblical situation is so different from the situations of today. For me, the key is in picturing again, seeing the truth happening among the people.

1. **Picture the problem with the truth.** One trick I do is to try to picture why this truth is a problem among them. Why do they need to hear this sermon anyway? Where is this biblical truth happening – or not happening – among them?

For example, in thinking about David and Goliath, why is this sermon needed? The reason is that there are many in the church who are facing what seem like Goliaths, situations that frighten

41

and overwhelm them, that seem unbeatable. In my preparation, I get specific in my thinking. I try to picture images of those David-like people in the congregation. Mary is facing cancer and the pain of it. Bill is fighting to keep his job, but it seems like a losing cause. Wanda and Dick are drifting apart and they wonder if their marriage can be saved, or if it is worth saving. Tom is so depressed. Life is hard on him and nothing seems to help him feel better. I'm sure that in your congregations, you know people who, like David, are facing "giants." Think about them specifically. Picture their needs and struggles. Can you see them? In the sermon, while I won't mention names specifically, I will certainly paint pictures of the kind of giants that they are facing. As I apply the truth, the sermon might say:

> Some of you can identify with David. You seem to be facing a Goliath. How tall, how frightening he appears! How in the world can he be defeated? For some of you it is a terrible sickness like cancer, or heart disease, or AIDS. The prognosis is not good. What can you do? Some of you are trying to make ends meet, but the job might end. How will you survive? Some are fighting to keep your marriage together and how hard that is. Is there a way through the hurt and pain, a way back to love and joy? For some of you, life has been hard and you have been knocked down so many times you are not sure it is worth trying to get up anymore. Depression is your constant companion. It never seems to end. Is there anything you can do in the face of it?

As I was writing that, faces were in my mind, the faces of Mary, Bill, Wanda, Dick, and Tom. In my mind's imagination, I saw them struggling with their giants. Then I described their situations, the giants that roamed their lands and threatened them. I have discovered in preaching that as I describe such problems briefly, many others relate to them. We all share the same common problems of life. I have also discovered that even though I might not mention people's specific "giant," they can still identify with the idea and place their problem into the sermon. As we picture the problems, the truth comes alive for them.

How would the Micah passage be applied? As I understand the problems of the text, there was injustice, the poor were being mistreated and ignored. There was a lack of kindness, no one seemed to care for another. There was pride, too much dependence on their own cleverness and ability with no dependence on God. Do these same problems exist today? Do people live unrighteously now?

> Unrighteousness! We don't live that way, do we? That was them, but not us. Is that so? Why is it that we do not really trust our leaders to tell us the truth? Why do the haves still take advantage of the have-nots? Why do the rich get better health care than the poor? Why do homeless people sleep on our streets and hungry people die each day in our world? Why are children abused and decent people mugged on the streets and marriages fall apart at alarming rates? Why do we have a world where trust in God is a rarity and to be a disciple brings ridicule and criticism? Why are our churches splitting and our ministers frustrated? Something is wrong! Could it be that we are not living the way we should? Maybe unrighteousness has invaded our world. Micah's time is not so different from our own.

I sought to picture the situations where unrighteousness prevailed and then paint word pictures of those situations. I wanted to help the people see the wrong that was around. The more specific, the better. We face the situations ourselves. We face unrighteousness. Sometimes, we participate in it. Understanding Micah's time should not be too difficult for us.

In applying the story of the prodigal son, can we paint a picture of those who have rebelled against God, picture the results of that rebellion? We usually know such individuals. Can we picture their story?

> Some of you here today understand this prodigal son. You have played his part. There was that moment when

43

you rebelled against God, cried out that you wanted the freedom to live as you desired, and you didn't need any God in your life. So you left God behind and did what you wanted. You lived as you chose and enjoyed your freedom. But now you know! Looking back it has not turned out the way you dreamed. It did not bring you the inner joy you thought it would. And here you are – with your life in shambles around you. Behind you are broken marriages, lost jobs, wrecked health, no friends. Joy is nowhere to be found. Maybe it is time to face up to the truth. You blew it! When you left God behind, it was the biggest mistake of your life. Like that prodigal, you are miserable, lonely, confused. What can you do? Is there a way beyond all the pain and failure?

Do you "get the picture?" We need to imagine ourselves into the lives of the people. If we have walked among them as their pastor, we will know their needs and find it easier to apply the biblical truth to them. Everyone struggles with the truths of the faith. Picturing the struggle is part of preaching.

2. **Picturing the solution.** What will it look like if the people do what the sermon suggests? What difference would it make in their lives specifically? Can we picture that? How would their lives change if the word we preach was taken seriously?

We need to visualize the changes that might occur. For example, as we preach on challenging the difficult problems of the world, some of the changes might be easy to imagine. If we learn to share with one another, we can see hungry people fed. If we learn to let God take away our prejudices, then we can see people of all races with their arms around each other, working to make a better world for all. If we learn to be peacemakers, we can see fighting cease and weapons being destroyed. If we learn to trust the Spirit of Christ in our churches, then we can see churches where worship is alive, witnessing is important, caring for the needs of others is never neglected, and where the spirit of love is the characterization of the people. Can we imagine that? These are the dreams and visions we have of what can be – with God's grace. These are the pictures we hold in our minds. We must not let these pictures be forgotten. We must keep painting them so such dreams will always be sought.

Sometimes, when I am trying to visualize what good might happen specifically because of the sermon, I bring into the study the faces of some of the members. They are representative of the makeup of the congregation. Some are school teachers – if they took the sermon seriously, how would it change the way they taught? Some are sailors – how would they live out the sermon's message when they are out on ships at sea? Some are students – would they be different kinds of students if the sermon took root in their lives? Some are couples struggling with their marriages – how would this sermon help them? Some are dealing with terminal illness – would this sermon make a difference in the way they faced the pain and the uncertainty of that? Imagining specific people helps me to picture how the sermon idea might look if it was taken seriously.

To preach without notes, we must think in pictures and images. To do that, we must imagine these pictures or testify to what we see. Using the story of the prodigal son, we might apply the hope of the sermon like this:

> So you have made the important decision. You will throw yourself on the mercy of God. "Not worthy to be called a son." When you do, what will happen? You heard it in the story. What happened there will be true for you. God will come running to embrace you, forgive you, call you son or daughter again. There will be such joy on the face of God because you have come back. You will be welcomed! To be truthful, others may not welcome you. Former friends may avoid you. Many will talk about you behind your back. Some will not forgive you. But God will! What happened before is history. God is more concerned about what you will become than in what you have been. That's the gospel! Do you need it? Are you ready for it? God is waiting — and looking — ready to welcome you back home. Ready to throw a party for you, to celebrate the fact that you were lost, but now are found. Go on, join the party!

As always, we need to try to be specific in our applications. The gospel is applied to real life situations. If they trust God, they can learn to face the giants of life. If they trust God, they can live the right way and stand in opposition to the evil in the world. If they trust God, the sinful can be forgiven, the lost can be found. Sermon ideas must be applied. The purpose of the sermon is to let the truth of God happen again among the people. We preach with the belief that God's grace will take the message and apply it to the needs of the people – and lives can be changed. Sermons are not to be lessons on history, but a real word for living now. In looking back over my years of ministry, how exciting it is to remember those whose lives were changed because they trusted Christ to guide them. As I remember them, their faces parade before my mind. I recall experiences we shared together. They seem to come alive for me again. For a moment I celebrate again the joy that came to their lives when they trusted Christ. Preaching is seeing the pictures of lives changed and telling others about the pictures we see.

THE ILLUSTRATION AS PICTURE

I have heard that everyone loves a story. I do not know if that is true for everyone, but it is true for me. Especially when it comes to preaching. When I was growing up, what I remembered most about the sermons I heard was not the catchy phrases or the definitions of terms or the long-involved explanations of significant theological terms. I remembered the stories. They caught my attention and interest. Even now, I can still bring to mind stories and illustrations that I heard 30 to 40 years ago. Through my preaching years, many have said to me, "I don't remember much else that you said, but I'll never forget that story you told." I would suspect that most of you have heard similar words. Always people are reminding me of a story that I told in a sermon several years earlier. They still remembered it! I think that should tell us something about preaching. If people remember the stories that well, maybe we need to make them a major part of the sermon.

So enters the issue of illustrations. In this section, I will mean by illustrations short stories, anecdotes, picturesque glimpses into real life. I am aware that some homiletic teachers discourage the use of such material. Some of their concern is warranted. Illustrations can be misused. Sermons must not become a string of stories connected by nothing of substance in between. Illustrations must serve to throw light on the truth of the sermon. It must not take the place of good exegesis and explanation. Also, illustrations must illustrate the point clearly. I heard one preacher say that if he found a good illustration that week, somehow it was going to find its way into the sermon the next Sunday. That is not good. Illustrations should only be used if they underscore the specific truth of a sermon. We do not preach illustrations supported by some truth. We preach the truth that is supported by illustrations. There are a lot of good illustrations that are in my file that I have never used. I have not found a sermon where they would be a good "fit." Only use an illustration if it truly throws light on the sermon idea.

Then illustrations must be appropriate and in good taste. Some criticize "tear-jerker" stories, stories that seemed to be guaranteed to move the emotions. There are plenty of such heart-breaking stories around. One preacher said that he chose his illustrations on the basis of whether or not they will "get" to folk. In other words, bring tears. Never choose an illustration on that basis. The criteria for using such an illustration is to use them only if they honestly and effectively throw light on the truth preached. If it does not, avoid it like the plague.

Illustrations must also be believable. I heard a story about Napoleon coming upon a soldier who had lost an arm in battle and the Emperor praised him for his sacrifice. The soldier said, "For the Emperor I would willingly give both my arms." With that, he took a sword and cut off his other arm. A stirring illustration of sacrifice, until someone asked, "How did he do that?" A good question. Such a scene would be hard to picture. Illustrations should be realistic and true to life. We do not want people thinking about an illustration, "Oh, come on! That can't be true!"

We need to use stories that are fresh. Some stories have been around so long they have grown long, gray beards. As soon as we start to tell the story, a collective groan is heard from the congregation. They have heard this story so many times before!

Try to avoid such illustrations. We must continually be on the lookout for new illustrative material, through our reading, listening, observing, and through our own experiences.

Used properly, illustrations are a tremendous aid to communication. The plus of illustrations is that they are easily pictured. What does the truth we preach look like in action? Stories help us see. For preaching without notes, this is vital. As we see the story taking place, as we imagine it in our minds, what we then do is to describe it to the people. Like the biblical stories, we need to put ourselves "into" the story, to stand again on the sidelines and watch it happening. Then we become eye witnesses to the story. When we preach it, we are just testifying to what we saw. Do we need notes for that? I don't think so.

Stories are helpful for preaching because they can involve the people in the sermon. Illustrations are non-threatening, as other people are doing the acting. The congregation can "overhear" the story, and if they chose, can put themselves into it wherever they think they fit. Also, a well-chosen story can appeal to the interest and to the total personality of the hearer. Stories can touch the mind and heart and will. They can be powerful motivators to action.

How can we best use stories in preaching without notes?

1. **Personal stories.** For years in preaching the use of personal stories was taboo. The sermon was to be about the truth of God, not about the preacher. The fear was that the sermon would be filled with too many "I's" and the eyes of the people would be taken off the Lord. Sermons were not to be personal. In recent years that emphasis has changed. We have realized that we can never take the personal element out of the sermon, even if we do not use personal stories about ourselves in them. Phillips Brooks was right about preaching being the truth presented through "personality." When we preach a sermon, we are in it. All the experiences of our lives that have made us who we are enter into it. Our feelings, our fears, our prejudices, our struggles, our hopes are in it. Our backgrounds influence the sermon and color our viewpoints, matters such as race and gender and our environment matter. Then, too, the truth of the sermon should have impacted our lives in some way. How has God used the sermon truth with

48

us? What have we done with it? We have a story and there are times when our stories are the best illustration of God's story. As I tell my students, before we can preach the sermon to others, we ourselves must first stand under the text. It needs to be a significant word to us before it can be a significant word to others. If the truth does not matter to us, it probably will not matter to anyone else when we preach it.

We must not shy away from the use of personal stories in our sermons. However, there are dangers we must avoid. We must not tell stories that make us out to be heroes or "Superman-like" Christians. I have heard preachers talk about taking a plane trip and by the time the plane landed, it seemed as if they had led everyone on the plane to the faith. Or those who always have the right word to "fix up" a struggling marriage or someone's confusing situation. Such stories can make us feel inadequate. Why can't we be as dedicated or as insightful? Such stories set up impossible standards for us to follow. How can we ever imitate them? Such examples can depress us. Since we can not do as they can, why try? We must never forget that serving Christ is hard and we are not always successful in what we try to do. Sometimes the stories should point out our failures and conflicts and doubts. We must not be afraid to show our vulnerability. If we are able to accomplish some good, it is due to the grace of God and not our cleverness.

We must never embarrass our spouses or our children in our stories. The best rule is never to use them as illustrations, especially in the churches that we serve. Nor should we ever violate confidences given to us in counseling or in the pastoral relationship. If we ever use a story involving another person in the church family, always get permission first. As a general rule, however, do not use stories with such people.

In preaching without notes, the value of telling our own stories should be obvious. We were there when the experience happened and all we do in preaching is to tell what happened to us. Can't we do that without notes? I had a friend who was involved in a car accident and told a hilarious and moving story of all that had happened to him. He told of the man asking him, as he lay on the highway waiting for the ambulance, "What do you think of your

49

God now?" There was the bumpy ride to the hospital, the doctor who mistook him for another patient and almost treated him in the wrong way, the nurse who asked him what that cross necklace he was wearing meant to him. It was a moving and engaging story. Then I heard him preach about it. Sadly, he had written it down and read it, word for word. It was boring! Gone was the excitement and energy and the mood changes he had shown when he first told the story to me. It had lost its "fire." I wanted to go up to the pulpit and tear the notes away from him and say, "You lived it! Tell me about it!" He said later that he was afraid he would forget the story. But how could he? He had already told the story over and over again to friends. There was no way he would forget!

In preaching, we *tell* our stories to the people, not read them. They are pictures in our minds. Trust the pictures! We are in the pictures. In a way, we used our mental cameras and took them. In our preaching, we develop these pictures for others to see. These personal experiences take the truth of God and brings it to life in actual experiences. The people will see how we deal with God. They can see that we understand their struggles because we have them ourselves.

In a sermon that sought to lead the people to trust God in their difficulties, I told this personal story:

> In 1979, I was in DePaul Hospital in Norfolk (VA). I had two kidney stones. All I can say about them is that they really hurt. Some of you know what I am talking about. They tried to get them to pass on for a few days. One did, but one did not. So they decided to cut it out. I was not overly happy about that decision. The night before the scheduled surgery, I was alone. My wife had gone home. An orderly had come in to go through the "preparations" for surgery, not a very joyous time. When he left, I was alone, fearful of what the next day would bring, feeling a bit sorry for myself, wondering where God was at the moment. DePaul is a Catholic hospital and in each room on the wall is a crucifix, a small statue of Christ hanging on the cross. The cross was so positioned that as I lay there in

50

the bed, I was looking right at it. In that moment, in the midst of the pain and self-pity, I began to think to myself. I was suffering, but one thing I felt – Jesus understood my pain because He had suffered pain on the cross. Somehow I knew that my pain was nothing compared to the pain that He experienced. Then the thought hit me! If someone had offered me a pill to take away the pain, I would have swallowed it in a second. Anything to stop the pain! But Jesus could have stopped His pain! He had the power to come down from the cross and leave it behind. But He didn't do it! Instead, He stayed on the cross and suffered the pain and death of it. Why? Because of me! He loved me that much and would not flee the pain to save Himself. He would suffer it to save me. In that moment, I was overwhelmed by a tremendous sense of the love of God. I felt that God was really there in that room, watching over me, staying with me. I would not be left alone! Somehow I began to know that whatever happened to me the next day – no matter how terrible – it would be all right. I would be able to face it because I knew, I really knew, I was loved by God. That love would never let me go. A feeling of peace came over me and I fell off to sleep, grateful for the love of God that surrounded me.

Many who had been in the same hospital shared with me after this sermon that they had experienced similar feelings as they viewed the crucifix on the wall. The cross had become a reminder to them of the love and care of Christ. This often happens with the sharing of personal experiences. Others identify with them and somehow, our story becomes theirs.

Sometimes our stories can be humorous and insightful. I once preached a sermon in which I was seeking to make the point that we must never underestimate what God will do with what we give. God will take what we give and use it far beyond our expectations. I told of this experience:

One afternoon, I was walking through the lobby of the Norfolk General Hospital when I heard my name being

51

called. From across the lobby a man came running toward me and said, "Hi, Dr. Litchfield, remember me?" Now I have to admit to you that of all the questions in life that I hear, that is not one of my favorites. As I stammered and stuttered, he began to tell me his story and I began to recall him. About ten years earlier he had visited our church for a couple of Sundays. When he came, his life was in a mess. He was in trouble with the Internal Revenue Service over taxes and was facing a possible jail term. Because of that worry he had begun to drink and had become a slave to the bottle. Because of that, he was about to lose his wife and family. He was in desperate shape. He then said to me in that lobby, "I want to thank you." "For what?" "One Sunday you preached a sermon about taking responsibility for our lives, not to blame what we become on somebody else. God used that sermon to speak to me. That afternoon I got down on my knees and prayed to God and promised to take responsibility for my life. With God's help, I did. Since that time, life has been great. I got out of trouble with the IRS, I became the master over the bottle, my marriage is better than ever. I want to thank you."

As he left me standing there, I was overwhelmed by what he had told me. I also wondered, if my sermon had meant so much to him, why did he go and join another church? But I let that thought pass. But such experiences amaze me, encourage me, humble me. It also made me curious. When I went back to the office, I dug down into my sermon files to get out that sermon that had meant so much to him. Early in my ministry, on Monday morning I would jot down a phrase or two at the top of my sermon manuscript as to how I felt the sermon had gone on Sunday. For that sermon, I glanced at what I had written. "Dead in the water! No one listened! A waste of time!"

I don't do that anymore. I have learned something along the way. If we offer faithfully to God what we have, somehow it will be used in magnificent ways. We must never underestimate what God will do with what we give.

52

Whenever I tell such stories, I re-live them. I have no trouble feeling the moods, picturing the setting, seeing all the faces. I was there! I lived those moments! In my preaching, I just "testified" to what I had experienced. I had no trouble getting involved in the delivery of them. Haven't you had such exciting experiences? Doesn't it excite you to tell others about them? In listening to student sermons, sometimes they go along in a slow, steady, monotonous pace. But then they start to tell of an experience they had, and everything changes. They become more animated, more natural, more personable. You can watch their fellow students perk up and listen more intently. They were telling the story about what they had experienced and usually, they did not use notes for that. When we tell our own stories in the sermon, I have a feeling the same thing happens to us and to our hearers. We get involved in the sharing of them and the sermon catches fire and comes to life. That is the value of a personal story.

2. **The stories of others.** Life is full of stories, stories that capture the truth in action. One of the assignments I give to students is to develop an illustration file of the stories they discover. Where do they get them? From everywhere! From their reading – of novels, poetry, history, newspapers, theology, sermons. They get them from watching TV and the movies, from observing the actions of others, from the sermons of other preachers, from music of all kinds. They get them from seeing and experiencing all the arts. They get them from life! As we go through life, we need to develop what I call the "homiletic eye," the ability to see the truths of God illustrated everywhere. The pictures are there if we will be sensitive to them. (By the way, it is good to put these illustrations into some good filing system. If we don't, we will probably lose them. It is also good to reference them with the author, book or place where it was found, date, any page numbers. If we ever need to produce an illustration for someone, such a file will make it easier to do).

To make such illustrations effective, we need to imagine them happening in our mind's eye. Like the biblical stories, we need to put ourselves into the scene. Hopefully, when we first read or saw or heard the illustration, it was meaningful to us. It spoke to us and moved us. So we collected it for our files. In the right sermon, we will use it, and because it has already been meaningful to us, we will find it easier to tell.

When we think of the illustration, imagine the action happening again. See the people moving, or smiling, or crying. Hear the words being spoken anew. Try to "live" that story in the imagination. We might speak the story out loud several times until we feel we can tell it confidently, without the use of notes. We picture it happening, and then tell others what we see.

The right illustration can be a powerful tool of communication. Stories are full of descriptive language, as opposed to mere prose. Such language helps picture the idea. Sermons can (and will) contain both prose and poetry. We must decide the best language for the moment. For example, a sermon that seeks to encourage people to persevere in their faith, never to quit holding on to it, can be concluded with the use of prose language.

> So here it is! We must always persevere in our discipleship, always going on, no matter what. Sure, we will face disappointment, criticism, frustration, maybe even pain. But we must not let it stop our service. When we are knocked down, we must get up and go on! Never quit! Never stop! Hold on and go on! Persevere! It is the way of discipleship.

Such a conclusion can be very effective. However, instead of that kind of exhortation, the point can be made through the use of this story:

> There was a B movie entitled *Hard Times Texas*. It was about a town named Hard Times. It was an apt name. The town was going strong for a while, but the town drunk burned everything down one night. After that, everybody moved away, except the town sheriff. He would go and stand at the town limits every day and whenever somebody would pass by, he would stop them and say, "I've got a dream. We can rebuild this town. It can be a great place to live. Will you help me rebuild it?" He did that over and over until he finally got enough people to believe in the

54

dream, and they rebuilt the town. When they did, all the former residents moved back, including the town drunk, who proceeded to burn down the town again. People packed up and left, all except that old sheriff, who went and stood by the town limits and would stop people passing by and say, "Hey, I have a dream. We can build a great town here. I know we can. Will you help me?"[1]

What we need to do is to stand up in this world, stop people and say, "Hey, we have a dream. We can build a world that can be a great place to live, where there is peace and goodwill to all. Will you help?" Maybe if we will do that long enough, always trusting God, we will find others ready to help us. Who knows? Maybe we can rebuild this world like God wants it. Will you help, and keep on helping?

Illustrations like this are plentiful if we keep our eyes and ears open. We should not be afraid to use the stories of others. However, we must be honest in the use of them. We must never tell about another's experience as if it were our own. We must always give credit where credit is due. Most of the time, we can simply say. "I read about . . ." or "I heard about the story . . ." Or we can easily identify the person by saying, "Billy Graham told the story of . . ." or "Billy Graham told about the time when he . . ." Such phrases protect the integrity of the story and do not harm the flow of the sermon.

Illustrations help to show in picture language what the truth looks like in action. When we see the story happening in our minds, all we do is describe that picture to the people. In our daily conversations we do that all of the time. We are always telling others about what we have seen or read or heard. We just need to take that storytelling ability into the pulpit. When we do, people will probably say to us, "I don't remember all that much of what you said, but I won't forget that story."

TELLING THE STORIES

One of the major keys to preaching without notes is the ability to put the sermon together in pictures, pictures that we see happening in our imaginations. We picture the biblical scenes, we picture the truth coming to life among the people through application, and we picture the truth in action through the stories of others. A major part of the sermon will contain such pictures, pictures that become stories, stories that involve characters and action and plot. It becomes like a mini-motion picture. Usually after seeing a movie, someone will ask me to tell about it. So I remember the movie and describe it. I tell about the plot and unfold it in its proper sequence. I highlight the major points of the movie. All the while, I am remembering the movie pictures in my mind. This is what we want to try to do with our sermons. We need to see them as movie clips – clips of the Bible in action, of our people living out that truth, of stories of that truth in action. As we seek to put the "clips" or pictures in sequence, the sermon begins to develop. What we then do in our delivery is to tell the people about the "movie" that we have seen. Hopefully, the pictures will be so real and fresh to us that we will not have much difficulty telling about it. In the next chapter, I will seek to show how to put such a sermon together through the use of an image outline.

Preaching without notes involves telling others about the stories we see. Preachers are story tellers, telling God's story in such a way that it will become the story of our people. To do this, we filter God's story through our story and the stories of others. We must work to develop the ability to *tell* stories. Are there any helps for that?

1. **Choosing the story.** In the process of developing the sermon, many stories will come across our paths. The problem will usually not be a lack of picture images, but which ones to use. What are the criteria for selecting the best stories?

    A. **Choose stories/pictures that we like.** Do we feel good about the story? When we first encountered it, did it reach out and "grab" us? Move us? Challenge us? If the story made an impact on us, then it will be easier to remember and tell to others. If we like the story, we will be excited about passing it on in the sermon.

    B. **Choose a story that we believe in.** By that I mean a story that we honestly feel illustrates well the truth we are preaching. From all the possibilities that we have to choose from, this story pictures it best. It is on the mark. We will tell the story with confidence because we know that it will throw great light on the idea. If it helps us to grasp the idea, then it will help others to do it.

C. **Choose a story that is easy to remember.** Practice telling the story out loud four or five times. Is it easy to remember? Or do we still have trouble recalling it? If so, it may be too difficult or too involved to use. Good stories have a natural flow to them that makes them easier to remember. If it is hard for us to keep in mind, it will be even harder for our people to follow. How easy is it to picture this story in our minds? Seek the clearest picture possible.

2. **Learning to tell the story.** Some people just can not tell stories. Maybe you know someone who, for some strange reason, can never tell a joke. That person always seems to botch the punch line, or forget important matters, or deliver it badly. Storytelling is an art. It is a craft to be learned. We pay good money in our society to go and hear good storytellers. How can we become good ones?

A. **Eliminate the unnecessary.** In telling a story, we must clearly understand the point of it and tell it so that the point will be strongly emphasized. We do not want anyone to miss that point. We must seek to eliminate unnecessary details or descriptions that will only confuse the picture. What is important to this story, what is not? Like a skilled surgeon, we must take a knife and cut away all useless tissue.

I had a friend tell of the time when he found a purse on the street that was full of a great deal of money. But he had trouble getting that point across. He said, "On Monday, or was it Tuesday? Oh, I think it was Monday, I was driving down Cliff Avenue – wait a minute – it might have been 26th Street! Anyway, it was about 9:30 in the morning – or was it 10:00? I'm not real sure. I was going to the grocery store, or maybe I was headed for the doctor's office . . . I was going about 25 or 30 miles an hour. There was not a lot of traffic on the street that day, a pretty day to go

57

for a drive, and I was listening to WCAB – wait, it could have been WSSD . . ." By this time, we are screaming, "Get on with the story. Tell us about finding the purse!" All that detail he presented was irrelevant and confusing. It drew out the story and made it difficult to follow. He needed to cut to the important matters – finding the purse, how much money was in it, and what did he do after he found it.

Sometimes when we tell our stories, we can get that detailed. So when getting ready to tell one, the first thing we have to do is to decide what is necessary and what is not. What details are needed to get the story across? Here is an illustration. As you read it, what do you feel is necessary detail, and what is not?

It was Christmas Eve, 1969. I was going to visit Ella, a 91-year-old church member, at the Smith Nursing Home in Ft. Worth, Texas. It was a cold, dreary day. I walked into the home about 4:30 in the afternoon, sort of tired from having so much left to do before Christmas Day. There were many residents sitting in wheelchairs in the hall. Christmas decorations were hanging everywhere. I reached the dark and dingy-looking ward where Ella was, along with three other patients. She had been a member of the church for a long time, and her family consisted of a son and daughter-in-law and two grandchildren. I made my way to the bed, reminded her of who I was, and started to carry on a conversation. We talked about how she was doing, and then I asked if her family was coming to see her. She replied, "I think they are going to come to see me on Christmas." When she said that, all of a sudden the woman in the next bed began to sing out loud. I didn't know her or her situation. She started to sing, "Silent Night, Holy Night." She had a scratchy voice that cracked several times as she made her way through the verses. And she was loud, so loud that I could not continue to carry on my conversation with Ella. So we just listened as the woman

58

struggled through the song. Finally, she stopped. I was relieved. I turned to look at Ella and I saw tears running down her cheeks. "Ella, are you all right?" "Fine," she said. Then she added these words. "Wasn't that just beautiful?" Suddenly I began to understand. There in that dark and dingy nursing home ward, in that place of loneliness and suffering, somehow the presence of God had come. Through the song sung with a scratchy and cracking voice, the hope of Christmas had come alive to Ella. So for a brief moment in that place, Christmas happened – for Ella, for that unnamed woman, even for me. God had come and even there, hope was alive.

This was an experience that I faced. It was very moving to me. But in this form, it becomes a very long and involved story with a lot of unnecessary details. The exact time and place did not really matter. The type of day it was outside, the wheelchairs and decorations, even the age of Ella are not needed. Nor did we need to know the length of time she had been a member of the church or the specific makeup of her family. This story could lose a lot of those details and still be effective. How would you retell this story? I did it this way:

It was late in the afternoon on Christmas Eve and I had one more stop to make, to visit Ella in the nursing home. As I walked into her ward, it was dark. Some of the other patients there were moaning. It seemed like such a lonely, desolate place. Despair felt like it was in the air. I began to talk with Ella. She told me that her family would probably come to see her on Christmas day. When she said the word "Christmas," it must have sparked a memory for the woman lying in the next bed because she began to sing in a loud, scratchy and cracking voice, "Silent Night, Holy Night." We stopped to listen to her sing. She finally stopped and I have to admit, I was glad. Then I noticed Ella. Tears were streaming down her cheeks. "Are you all right, Ella?" "Fine," she replied. Then she added these words, "Wasn't that just beautiful?" All of a sudden, it hit me. It seemed to me that the lonely, desolate ward had become a hillside where a chorus of angels was singing. I began to understand. In that moment, in that place, Ella and the unnamed woman had thought of God and had again experienced the presence of God. The truth of Christmas happened again. In that place of despair, for Ella, that other woman, even for me, hope had come. And the darkness was no longer so dark.

We should streamline the stories we tell. Only the important and necessary details are included. Anything that does not contribute to the making of the point needs to be eliminated.

B. **Develop a sense of drama.** Good storytellers usually have a flair for the dramatic. They "feel" the drama of the story. They know when to speed up or slow down, what to emphasize and what to downplay, when to pause and when to go on, when to be funny and when to be serious. They understand the moods of the story. They seem to "lose" themselves in the story.

I hope we can do that. Can we feel the tension and drama of the story? Can we capture that drama in our storytelling? As a general rule, the less important material we speak faster, and we slow down for the more important matters. A pause is a good way to emphasize and highlight a point. We can highlight the point with a pause either before or after it. The silence of a pause is a good emphasizer. We should work to understand and feel the moods of the story. If it is funny, we should display joy. If it is sad, we should convey sorrow. Stories are not to be told "matter-of-factly." We need to lose ourselves in them. The goal is to let the story get inside us.

A good way to discover the drama of a story is to practice it out loud. Get somewhere where no one can hear you and think you have gone crazy. But speak the story aloud several times. Try to feel it, to picture it. Be overly dramatic as you speak it, and try to listen to how it sounds. I think that you might begin to sense the flow of the story, the moods of it, the important parts of it. Practicing

60

stories out loud will help us understand how to tell it. Try this practice and see if it does not help. I have found it quite useful.

C. **Develop a sense of timing.** A story moves to a climax, the big point. Everything we do is to lead to that point. The people must not miss it. We must bring them to the "punch line" and highlight it. Usually, we speak more slowly when we get to the climax. Speak distinctly, clearly. The climax is the "wow" of the story, the truth that "slaps them in the face." We must not rush over it or pass it too quickly. I find it helpful to pause right after I bring home the punch line of a story, giving the people more time to absorb the idea, to experience the impact of the point. Pace the telling of the story so that it leads up to the climax and then let the truth "explode" to them.

We can develop our storytelling abilities. The best way to do that is to practice the telling of stories. We need to tell them at every chance we get and continually check ourselves against the list given above. Do we deal with the essentials of a story? Do we feel the drama of the story, lose ourselves in it? Are we developing a good sense of timing in our delivery? One good way to check how we are doing is to tell stories to children at bedtime (if we have them). We have two choices. We can read them a story, or we can tell it to them enthusiastically. If we want them to go to sleep we should probably read the story to them. But when we tell it to them, they usually get so involved in the story that it excites them and they end up wide awake. If we can keep their interest, we are probably telling the story well. By the way, there might be an analogy to preaching there. If we want our people to go to sleep, read them our sermons. If we want to get them involved and excited about the sermon, tell it to them. Such is the value of preaching without notes.

The children's sermon is another place where we can practice the telling of stories. It is my judgment that most people do not know the biblical stories anymore. One way to correct that is to use the children's sermon time to retell the great stories of the Bible. Children love stories and learn through them. Can we tell them the stories in such a way that we keep their interest? Can we get involved in the telling of them? Can we get excited about it?

The more we tell the stories that we have pictured in our minds, the easier it will get. Don't be discouraged if you find storytelling difficult at first. Keep at it and I feel you will develop more effective skills to do it. And we never quit learning and improving. Learning the art of storytelling is a lifetime work.

RECAP

We have covered a lot of ground in this chapter. The concept of picturing is vital to preaching without notes. As I hope you noticed, over and over again I kept saying that we must picture the idea in our minds and then tell the people what we see. You probably got tired of my saying it. But I did it for a purpose. We must develop the ability to see. We need to try to see the biblical text come to life. It will not be just words on a page, but real events happening again, real pictures being formed in our imaginations. Through the picturing of the biblical material, we help explain the meaning of the text, the meaning of the Word of God.

We must also picture the application of the truth to our people. The biblical idea is not to be just information, but a truth that can be experienced and faced today. In applying the idea, I suggest that we imagine how it is a problem with the people and then how it can be a solution for them. Picture the need and how the biblical truth meets that need.

Throughout the sermon, we will interweave the explanation and application of the sermon idea. One tool to help us do that is illustration. Our stories or the stories of others can underline and throw light on the subject. The good thing about such illustrations is that they are really pictures in action. We imagine them in our minds, and then we testify to others about what we see.

Learning to tell stories is a must for preaching without notes. We need always to be practicing that at every opportunity we can. Losing ourselves in the story is helpful. If we can become part of the story, what we do is then describe what we see.

In constructing our sermons, we need to concentrate on putting them together like one would do a movie, one scene naturally leading to the next one, one picture leading to another picture. There are three major backdrops for the scenes – the biblical situation, the present situation, and the situation of the illustration. These pictures need to be arranged in proper sequence, each building upon the other. To preach without notes, we then seek to remember the scenes as they unfold toward the sermon climax.

It is time to think about how we might do that more specifically. How can we put the scenes together in such a way that they will not be hard to remember?

---

1. Edwin Muller, "Response to New Life – A View From Prison," Sermon: Riverside Church, New York, New York, 13 Jan. 1974, p. 9-10.

Chapter 4

Imaging: A Mural On The Wall

Once in a while, I will go to see displays of art. On one of these rare trips, I happened upon a mural that was painted on a wall. It was divided into several different scenes, each depicting a piece of the total picture. It brought to mind a stained glass window I had seen in a church. On it were several scenes that sought to display the life of Christ. There was the manger scene, His baptism by John, the Sermon on the Mount, the crucifixion, the Resurrection, the Ascension, and the Second Coming. Seven symbols — each denoting a part of the life of Jesus. When we put them together, we get a pretty good representation of the total life of Christ.

The mural on the wall was like that. Put all the separate pictures together and you got a representation of the whole idea of the painter. As I have thought about that scene, I have come to believe that a sermon can be developed like a mural on the wall. A good sermon can be pictured in individual images or symbols that, when put together, add up to the total sermon idea.

For example, suppose that we saw a mural on a wall that conveyed the major moments of the life of Abraham Lincoln. There would be a picture of a log cabin, some rails split by an axe, two people debating, the White House, a battle scene, the Emancipation Proclamation, Ford's Theater in Washington. Here are seven symbols that tell us about Lincoln. If we have done our homework and studied about his life, the symbols would not be hard for us to understand – or describe to others. The log cabin – a symbol of where Lincoln was born and grew up, often reading books by the light of the fire in the fireplace. The rails that were split – that was how Lincoln got the nickname "the Railsplitter," a reminder of how hard a worker he was. Two men debating – that refers to the famous Lincoln-Douglas debates over the issue of slavery, a debate that brought Lincoln into the national spotlight. The White House – a reminder that Lincoln was elected president. The battle scene – a grim reminder of the Civil War fought when he was President. The Emancipation Proclamation – the decree Lincoln presented that declared that from that moment on, slaves were free. Ford's Theater – a somber symbol of the fact that Lincoln was assassinated by Booth. All the symbols taken together help us put the life of Lincoln into proper focus. The symbols jog our memories and set loose pictures of his life. Once the pictures are set loose, what we then do is simply describe to others the pictures we see in our minds.

To me, when a sermon is finally finished, it can be pictured like a mural on the wall. It can be put down in symbols and images, images that jog our memories and set loose pictures about the sermon. Once we see the pictures, then we tell others about the pictures we see. We can understand the images "on the wall" because we have done our homework – on the biblical text, on the sermon idea, on the application of it today, on the illustrations that throw light upon that sermon idea. The sermon is captured in the images.

Now I hope you can understand why I stressed the importance of picturing the sermon. As we develop our pictures, the sermon comes to life. What we need to do with the pictures we have is to try to condense them down to a symbol or image, one we can write in a word or two. A metaphor, if you please, of the idea.

One of the major emphases in preaching today is on the use of the metaphor. Preachers need to use "metaphorical language." Warren Wiersbe, in his recent book *Preaching and Teaching With Imagination*, defines metaphor as a "verbal transfer that connects two seemingly unrelated things and creates from this union something new."[1] So Jesus said that He was a "door" (John 10:9). That is not literally true, but it is metaphorically. It symbolizes the truth that Jesus opens up the way to God. To get to God, we need to go through that door, which is Christ. The metaphor of "door" is a picturesque image and helps people "see" Christ as the way through which they must travel to God.

Wiersbe states that in using metaphorical language, we "turn ears into eyes and help them see the truth."[2] Somehow, that is what I have been trying to say. We need to think in pictures and then describe the pictures to our listeners. To help us remember the pictures, we can try to think of them in terms of metaphors, similes, or images. This is vital if we are going to preach without notes.

A CONTROLLING METAPHOR

In working with students, I try to get them to develop an overarching metaphor for their sermon. If they had to describe their sermon in an image, what would it be? Robert Hughes, a teacher of preachers, writes about having a "controlling image" as the heart of the sermon:

> "These images, usually introduced at the outset of the sermon, come back again and again to give unity to the sermon."[3]

Such an image can capture the essence of the sermon for the hearers. If they can remember the metaphor or image, they will remember the sermon. Once I preached a sermon titled, "When Fighting Green Tigers." What in the world is a green tiger? When one of my children was young, he began waking up in the middle of the night, terrified by a dream or nightmare. It was always the same. He would see a green tiger staring at him. He was scared, fearing the tiger wanted to eat him. After several nights of this, and tired from getting up so much, I fell back on all my seminary training and my knowledge of psychology and counseling and decided to try something. In other words, I was desperate and was willing to try anything. I took a stab at an idea. I asked him what the tiger did in the dream. "Nothing," he said. "He just sits there and looks at me." "You know what," I said, "I think that tiger is looking for a playmate. It's lonely and wants a friend. The next time you see the tiger, ask it if it wants to play with you, to be your friend." To my utter surprise, it worked! He never woke up again with that dream. I used that image as a metaphor for fear and preached about dealing with our fears, that we can not run from them, but must face up to them. Who knows? Maybe when we do, we will discover that the fears were not worth fearing. But we need to face up to those "green tigers." For several weeks after that sermon, I had quite a number of people come and say to me that they wanted to talk about their "green tigers." The metaphor stayed with them.

One of the exercises I do sometimes is to read the obituary column. I think I do it to find out if my name is there. If it isn't, I guess I'd better get on with my life. But obituaries are very revealing. In a few brief words, they sum up the major accomplishments of a person's life: what he did, any major achievements and awards, family history, church affiliation, if any. I sometimes find it quite encouraging to read the great things some people have done with their lives. One morning I was reading through them and I came upon the name of a man who had lived for 77 years. When they summed up his life, it was captured in one, brief sentence. "He was a member of the Lake Wright Golf Club." That was it! Nothing more was said about him. I thought to myself, what a waste that was. Here was a man who was given 77 years of life and when others looked back over it, the highest achievement they could think to say about it was that he had belonged to a golf club. It seemed like such a waste of a life. All that he might have done with it – helping others, coaching young people, serving God through a church, having a strong family. But when he was remembered, it was for a golf membership. Then I wondered about us. Do we do any better? That led to a sermon on the rich man in the Bible, so wealthy and successful, with so much ability to do much good for others and for his community. But all he would be remembered for was that he had a lot of barns. I entitled the sermon, "A Member of the Golf Club," and that became a metaphor for the kind of life we live and what we make of it.

This is how the controlling metaphor works. It is a peg upon which we can hang the basic sermon idea. It can also serve as a glue that ties that sermon together. Basic moves or point changes can be indicated by the use of the metaphor. The value of the image is that it puts into "picture form" the basic truth of the sermon and helps people to see it.

Often the Bible can serve as the source for the controlling metaphor of the sermon. The text might yield the image for us. So the giant Goliath becomes a metaphor for all the struggles of life that we have to face that seem unbeatable. Or Micah's call to righteousness can fall under the idea of "Requirements for Living." The story of the prodigal son is crammed with tasty metaphors — the far country as a symbol of our rebellion against God; the pig sty as a symbol of the results of that rebellion; home as an image for the forgiveness of God; the robe and shoes and ring serve as symbols of acceptance into God's family; the final party as a symbol of the joy we will know in God's kingdom. In dealing with the text, we need to be sensitive to the metaphors, for they may be the images around which we can build our sermons.[4]

Here are some of the biblical metaphors I have used in some sermons:

"The Angel on a Rock" – a symbol of the triumph of Christ on Easter. (Matthew 28:2)

"Seeing the Face of God" – a sermon that dealt with what God was like, based on the moment when Jacob met Esau again and said that to see his face was like seeing the face of God. (Genesis 33:10)

"Gethsemane: A Struggle of Wills" – dealing with the difficult choice between doing what God wants or we want. (Matthew 26:36-46)

"A Tale of Two Bowls" – contrasting the bowl that Jesus used to wash the disciples' feet with the bowl Pilate used to wash his hands and deny responsibility for the crucifixion. (John 13:25; Matthew 27:24-26)

"The Empty Tomb" – a sermon on the resurrection. (John 20:1-9)

"Sermon From a Donkey" – the donkey serving as a metaphor for the message Jesus was seeking to convey by riding into Jerusalem on it during that Palm Sunday. (Luke 19:28-38)

The possibilities are endless. The Bible is a book loaded with images and metaphors that cry out to be preached. We must keep our eyes open for them.

A FORMULA

To preach without notes, we need to picture the sermon in symbols and metaphors. I have developed a formula that I think will help us do that. As we seek to "plot" the sermon, I feel it will come in handy. The formula is this:

IDEA to PICTURE to IMAGE

1. **Idea.** This comes from the information developed with the cover page. The idea is the thesis and objective of the sermon and how it is to be developed. The idea is the truth that we want to say, the foundation of the sermon.

2. **Picture.** How can that idea be presented clearly? Hopefully, we can put the idea into pictures. There is the picture of the text, what the idea in the text looks like in action. How can we help it be seen? Once we see the idea in the text, we seek to picture it taking place in the lives of the hearers, the idea being applied. We picture how the idea can be a problem for the people and then how it can be a solution for them. With the help of illustrations – our own or the stories of others – we try to bring the idea to life. We try to see it in pictures and then seek to tell the people what we see. I hope this all sounds like "old hat" because it has been the subject of the preceding chapters.

3. **Image.** As we think about the picture, can we get it down into an image of a word or two? For example, as we picture David battling Goliath and finally defeating him, can we picture that in an image or metaphor? Maybe we can use such images as "fallen giants" or "slingshot." When we think of those images, they remind us of the story of David. When they do, then we tell the story that we know, a story that explains and applies the idea. So the word, say "slingshot," becomes one of the images in our mural on the wall. Having put the idea into a picture story, the image simply "kicks" us into the story, reminding us of it. When we tell the story, the idea is presented in a memorable way. So all we really need in an outline is just the word "slingshot." That word becomes the key word that helps us recall the idea. To put the story of David into the outline formula, it would look like this:

IDEA	PICTURE	IMAGE
David killed the giant Goliath	David kills Goliath with a slingshot	Slingshot

The one word, "slingshot," reminds me of the story of David and Goliath.

When I tell the story that I picture in my mind, I explain the idea in the text, that David killed Goliath with God's help. If I wanted to develop the idea further in the outline, I would do it this way:

IDEA	PICTURE	IMAGE
David trusted God's power to help him defeat Goliath	David's trust	God's power

If I wanted to move from that section that explains the meaning of the text to a section on application, I would outline it thusly:

IDEA	PICTURE	IMAGE
We face giants	Giants of sickness, joblessness, divorce, depression	Personal giants

You may remember that in thinking of application for this idea, I had pictured the giants that certain people in the congregation were facing. I talked about the hard situations of Mary, Bill, Wanda, Dick, and Tom. Having seen their giants, in the sermon I will describe them. To remind me of this part of the sermon, the image "personal giants" will be what I need. Those two words will remind me of the giants that the people were facing. I then describe these "giants" that I can picture in my mind. When I do that, the idea begins to be applied to the people.

I hope this is not sounding too complicated. We get to this formula only after we have done our homework on the text, developed a clear focus and objective, and plotted out a plan for developing the idea, a plan that will help us accomplish our objective. We then have spent some time mulling over how we can picture the sermon – picturing the text and application. We have been thinking about possible illustrations to use that could help us paint the idea in a better light. After we have done all of that, then we start thinking about the formula. Through the use of it, we can begin to make a sketch of the way the sermon might go.

I want to try to illustrate the process throughout this chapter with a sermon that I call "A Word for Willie." Before I went to seminary, I taught the sixth grade for a year. In that class of 11-year-olds, there was a 15-year-old boy named Willie. He was a problem student, although a very likeable boy. He asked me a question one day at school. He wanted to know if I could tell him what was the "big deal" about Jesus, what was so special about Him? It was a sincere question, and a searching one. What could I say? What would anyone say? That experience caused me to try to develop a sermon that would answer Willie's question. What would be my – or our – word for Willie?

In wrestling with that idea, the text I landed upon was John 8:2-11. Now I know that passage was not included in many original manuscripts, but it did find its way into the translations we have today. I feel the stories of the New Testament seek to help us understand what it is that is so special about Jesus. In studying the text in John, I did not find it contradicting any idea about Jesus found in the rest of the Gospels. In fact, it underscored the uniqueness of Christ. I felt comfortable in using this text as the foundation for the sermon.

To make a long struggle short, I developed a cover page for the sermon:

Title: A Word for Willie
Text: John 8:2-11
Thesis: Jesus will do for us what no one else will.
GO: Evangelistic
SO: That they will trust Jesus to meet their every need.
Signposts:

I. Jesus will love us when no one else will.

II. Jesus will forgive us when no one else will.

III. Jesus will believe in us when no one else will.

After I had arrived at this road map, I began to mull over it and try to think about it in pictures. The text was a story with plot and action and characters. It was not too hard to imagine it happening. I thought about people who needed in their lives what Jesus brought to this woman. There are many who do not feel that even God could love them – and I thought about them and how this story could comfort them. I also know far too many who have a hard time believing forgiveness is real; they have made some terrible mistakes and think that they are unforgivable. How would the forgiveness of Jesus change them? And I know several who do not believe much in themselves and feel like the best days of their lives are behind them. The future looks bleak to them. Is there a word for them in this story? How would it change them?

In my mind, I began picturing people and events and actions that seemed to capture the essence of the biblical story. I then sought to recall some illustrative material about these ideas. I spent some time going through my illustration file, seeking to discover if there were some good stories about love or forgiveness or hope. I culled out some possibilities and put them in a pile on the desk.

After all of that, I was ready to begin trying to put the sermon together into an image outline. I was going to depend on the formula: IDEA to PICTURE to IMAGE. What was the process?

DEVELOPING THE OUTLINE

Brainstorming

The first thing to do is to take out some sheets of paper, usually one page per point or move or major division. It is time to do some brainstorming of the ideas and we need to write the ideas down. The idea here is to put down in a brief sentence any thought that we think might help us develop the idea. I would start with the idea about needing love, then move to the one about needing forgiveness, and so on. I am not trying to be logical or exact. I am just trying to think of anything that will help me communicate the idea before me. Such ideas have come from my study of the text, from picturing the application, and from any illustrative material that I may have found. What am I thinking about this idea? How can I "bring it home" to them? That is my motivation for the brainstorming.

IMAGING THE BEGINNING

For me, I begin with the beginning. How will I get into the sermon? How can I raise the issue in a way that will engage the hearers? How should I begin?

There are many teachers who feel that the introduction of a sermon should be among the last things written. But I do not agree. I need to develop a beginning that will lead naturally and smoothly into the body of the sermon. In a way, the introduction becomes a "front door" that leads me into the house. I must find the best way and right way in before I can tour the rooms. The truth is, if I do not go through the door, I do not get into the house.

In the same way, if our people do not go "through the door," they will not get into the "house," or into the core of the sermon. So I need to do some serious thinking to find the best way to get them through the door. I must construct a beginning that will keep their interest and attention. Notice I did not say "get" their attention. I feel if we enter the preaching moment respectfully, we will have their attention. When it is time to preach, we should go and stand in the pulpit and for the first few seconds, stand there quietly. Take a deep breath and slowly look at all the people. The silence will be "deafening" to them and they will soon be casting glances our way. When we feel we have their attention, then we speak. The hope of the introduction is not to gain their attention, but not to lose it. I had a woman in my church tell me one day, "To be honest, I listen to you for the first few sentences. If you don't 'grab me' and cause me to feel that you will talk about something that matters to my life, I will tune you out and go ahead and plan my supper menu for the next week." I didn't like her telling me that! After all the work I had put into a sermon, it seemed like she could have given me more than a few sentences! But after she told me that, whenever I began to develop a sermon beginning, her words rang loud and clear to me. How could I keep her from planning that menu?

I will be bold enough to venture the opinion that there are a lot of people like her in our pews. We must seek to engage them in a conversation with our sermon and we must do it quickly, or they will be "gone." Is our sermon about that which matters to them? Is it about life and its real needs? Will it touch them where they live? It is our hope that the beginning will do all of that.

In brainstorming how to begin my sermon on "A Word for Willie," I already had my starting point. My experience with Willie would be the story I told, that moment that led up to his asking me the question, "What's so special about Jesus?" Also, the metaphor I had developed for the sermon would come into play. How would I answer that question? What would be my "word for Willie"? The sermon would be my attempt to answer that question. So as I brainstormed the beginning I put down several phrases:
"Willie's question: What's so special about Jesus?"

"We must answer that question."

"Do we know how to answer him?"

"Will the answer matter to anybody in the congregation?"

"How would I answer it now?"

"Text: religious leaders, woman caught in adultery, Jesus – is there an answer here? Where?"

After brainstorming a while, I then seek to put the beginning together in what I hope will be a logical, interesting, and engaging manner. I thus outlined it, using the special formula:

IDEA	PICTURE	IMAGE
1. What is so special about Jesus?	Willie asked me, "What is so special about Jesus?"	Willie's question
2. Can we answer that question?	Do we have an answer?	Answer
3. What would be an answer for us?	Giving an answer	Word for Willie

| 4. Text: Religious leaders asked about the woman caught in adultery | Text story | Text |
| 5. How does the text answer the question? | Jesus' answer | Jesus' answer |

Now the ideas are just brief, summary statements. I have not yet written out the sermon. Instead, I have been thinking about the idea, often talking about it out loud. But for this outline, all I want is to have brief, capsule statements of the idea. Usually, each of these sentences will wind up as a whole paragraph in the fully-developed sermon.

The idea is further summarized in a picture. We imagine the idea coming to life. We further condense the picture into an image of a word or two. Here is an important point: when I do write the sermon at a later time, my writing will be of the picture part of the outline. The picture should capture the essence of the idea. It will describe it and help it be seen. Remember, to preach without notes we seek to develop pictures in our minds and then describe them to the people. When we do that, a major part of our language will be of the poetic, descriptive variety. I will have more to say about the writing of the sermon in the next chapter.

So the idea is forming. We have an image. The image reminds us of the picture. When we remember the picture and describe it, the basic idea will be preached. In essence, I have now gotten the beginning down into five brief images:

Willie's Question
Answer
Word to Willie
Text
Jesus' Answer

If I can remember these five images, then I should be able to describe the pictures they bring to mind. And, hopefully, I can describe the pictures without the use of notes. Learning the images is the key. They are our mural on the wall. If we memorize anything, memorize the images. They are tiny capsules of the whole sermon.

I want to try to show how this works. I want to go through the beginning of the sermon on Willie, giving you the images and sharing the text of the sermon.

Image one: "Willie's Question"

Before I went to seminary, I taught the sixth grade and in that class of 11-year-olds, there was a red-headed, freckle-faced 15-year-old boy named Willie. Willie was the kind of student who was always in trouble, always winding up in the principal's office. He was the kind of boy that, if he was absent, the day went by smoothly. But if he was there, it was a long, hard day. Not many had a good word for Willie. I wanted to understand him better, so I did some research about his life. I discovered that Willie was the product of a broken home, several times over. Throughout his life, Willie had been an abused and neglected child. Willie really felt that no one cared too much for him.

One day at recess, Willie came over to me. He knew that I would soon be headed off to seminary to study to become a preacher. He said, "I want to ask you something. All my friends say that what I need to do to solve my problems is to go to church and to believe in Jesus. I don't see why. I know these friends and believing in Jesus doesn't seem to do too much for them. Maybe you can tell me. What is so special about Jesus?"

Comment: This was the personal experience that led me to preach this sermon. It was a personal experience that I could easily picture and describe. The basic issue of the sermon was clearly and quickly raised by this story.

Image two: "Answer"

Well, what would you tell him? What would be your word for Willie? Maybe you wonder the same thing. You have heard about Jesus a lot and you hear others talking about how you need to believe in Jesus. But you do not know why. Why should you believe? Just what is it that is so special about Jesus?

Comment: This served as a transition move from the raising of the issue to connecting it with the people there. I wanted some to see that they were just like Willie in wondering about the question. I felt that there were several in the congregation who were searching for an answer to that question. The sermon was an attempt to meet that need.

Image three: "Word for Willie"

I want to tell you what I told Willie that day in the schoolyard. I want to give you my word for Willie, and for any of you who are asking that question. What is so special about Jesus? **Comment**: This "move" designates the direction that the sermon will take. It will seek to answer Willie's question, and therefore, answer the question for those in the pew.

Image four: "The Text"

In the story from the scripture, we can find the answer. The New Testament writers tried to tell us why Jesus was special through the stories they told. So we have this story. Here is the scene. Jesus was teaching the people and the religious leaders brought a woman to Him who had been caught in the act of adultery. There was no doubt about that. Now the Law of Moses dictated that those caught in adultery – both the man and the woman – should be stoned to death. These religious leaders were ready to carry out that sentence. But they made a mistake. They asked Jesus what He would do.

Comment: At this point, I relate the issue to the biblical material. It will serve as the basis for the answer to the question. My purpose here was to sketch briefly the scene and set it up for the rest of the sermon. Basically, I try to describe the textual scene as I picture it in my mind.

Image five: "Jesus' Answer"

What did Jesus do? As we see what Jesus did, we can begin to get an answer to our question.

What is so special about Jesus? Well, the first word I told Willie that day was this: Willie, Jesus is special because He will love you when no one else will. (This is the beginning of Point I)

Comment: The last image is simply a transition into the first point of the sermon. Transitions should be brief and direct us to the major signposts on our journey. I showed how I got into the first point. The metaphor describing my conversation with

Willie will be used throughout the sermon, especially when I come to the basic points of the sermon development.

This is the way that the image outline will hopefully work. The image we get will remind us of the picture, a picture which is a good description of the sermon idea. As we have developed the cover page with our sermon journey clearly focused, and then thought about the explanation and application of these ideas in pictures, we just need to get a word or two that summarizes the pictures we have. They become the images we put into the outline. Even if we do not preach without notes, if we can develop the images, all we need to take into the pulpit are the images. To see them is to be reminded of the pictures. And on it goes!

Begin with the beginning. Keep in mind that we want to accomplish three basic purposes in it. We want to raise the issue, relate the issue to the people, and then relate it all to the text. However the beginning is done, we want to do those tasks.

1. **Raise the issue.** One great help in starting a sermon is when it has a controlling metaphor. If it does, the unfolding of the meaning of the metaphor is a good place to begin. In the sermon on Willie, the metaphor – a word for Willie – is developed quickly. Most controlling metaphors can be done that way. In a sermon on David and Goliath, right at the beginning I need to unfold the meaning of "giants" as a metaphor for those difficult times we will face. If I do not, the sermon will not make sense to them. But once I have established the meaning of "giants," it is an image that the people can hold on to throughout the sermon – and after it.

Remember this: be direct in the introduction. Do not waste time. Get to the point! Reach out and bring the people into the sermon as quickly as possible. When we begin, we should seem to be running right up to the person and saying, "I've got something to tell you that can change your life!" The start of the sermon must bring them face to face with the issue. In a way, it sets out why they need this sermon, why it is important for them to listen. However we start, get to the heart of the matter directly.

2. **Relate the issue to the people.** As I have evaluated my sermons, I have discovered that the vast majority of them begin with a contemporary illustration that raises the issue. Such an

illustration is non-threatening, allowing the hearers to "overhear" the problem. After the story, it is usually an easy task to relate the point of it to them. Simple transitional questions or sentences should serve the purpose:

"Have you ever felt like that?"

"Can you understand that?"

"That sounds far too familiar, doesn't it?"

"Have you ever struggled with that problem?"

"I am afraid that most of us have had that experience."

"That story is a familiar one to us – for we have lived it – live it still."

The main need is to drop the idea into their laps and help them see that the sermon is going to be about an issue that affects them and their discipleship. In the sermon on Willie, I started with the illustration and then related it to the people with the question, "Well, what would you tell him?" That will hopefully start a dialogue with them that will be carried on throughout the sermon.

3. **Relate to the text.** Relating the idea to the text will tie us to the foundation for the sermon. We will be looking for an answer from the Word of God, and not from just our opinions. In essence, what we say in the sermon rises from scripture. As we have honestly wrestled with it, this is what we feel is its word. That is where our authority lies – in the scripture. We must strive honestly to weave the sermon from the strands of the biblical material. Bringing it in at the beginning will help us do that.

I repeat this word about the beginning. Be brief! The introduction is just the front porch that gets us into the house, or the aroma that draws us into the kitchen. We must not dwell too long on it. Two to three minutes should suffice. We start the sermon in the introduction. We do not turn on the engine and just rev the motor over and over again. Start it and get on going. Raise the issue, relate it to the people and the text, and then get on down the road.

IMAGING THE SIGNPOSTS

After the introduction, we then move to the development of the major steps of the sermon. They are the main moves, points, divisions in the sermon trip. They will lead us to the objective of the sermon.

1. **Brainstorming.** If we have separate divisions and sections, we can start brainstorming ideas that can help develop that particular section. The idea is to put down any and every thought that comes to mind as to how the section might be developed. I would suggest that we do it under three categories:

A. Brainstorming Explanation

How can we present the point we want to make from the text? For example, the first signpost of the sermon on Willie was this: Jesus is special because He will love us when no one else will. How is that idea presented in the text? How did I come up with it? What in the text led me to that conclusion? So I will brainstorm about that, recording the thoughts that come to mind. So I put down such thoughts

– Lack of love. Religious leaders wanted to stone her.

– Law. Both man and woman should be stoned. Where is the man here? Wonder if he was a Pharisee?

– She was used as a pawn to try to trick Jesus.

– No one seemed to care about her feelings.

– How alone she must have felt!

– Made a mistake. They asked Jesus about it.

– No answer for a while – wrote on the sand. Why?

– Jesus caused them to face their sin, so they left.

– Jesus defended her. Stood between her and the religious leaders. Saved her life.

– For people like her, Jesus came.

– He cared when no one else did. Went against the Law and the religious leaders.

All of these were thoughts that come to mind as I pictured the story happening. In a way, the sentences I put down described the action that was taking place. I really began to realize how much Jesus cared for this woman. He did go against the Law of Moses and against what the religious leaders wanted to do. I am sure it was risky business to do that. Evidently, she was more important to Jesus than the letter of the law or even

81

the approval of the religious establishment. I saw love there. He was the only one who had it. I felt like my point was legitimately there in the text and I could picture to the people how it was so.

Notice: at this point, I am just brainstorming the ideas. Later, I will select the ideas I want to use and arrange them in a logical sequence. For now, I just brainstorm.

B. Brainstorming Application

There are two areas of application to keep in mind. The first deals with the *problem*. Why do they need to hear about the love of Jesus? What problems do they have with that love? Why do they need this sermon idea? So the brainstorming:

– Hear about the love of Jesus all the time.

– Teenager: all I hear is that "Jesus loves me." I'm tired of it.

– Do we believe Jesus really loves us?

– Not sure we believe in God's love.

– We are often very unloving.

– Woman felt she did not deserve the love of God.

– God showed love in Jesus. Cross is the symbol of that great love.

– Man, active in church, thought he could earn God's favor.

– Love – not earned or deserved.

Some of the ideas I will use in the sermon. Some I will not. But for now, I put them all down and I will mull over them later when I organize the point more specifically.

After thinking about the problem side of application, I then brainstorm on the *solution* side of it. How will this idea of love be helpful for them? How will it make a difference in their lives? What do they need to celebrate about this love?

– Not deserved. Does not have to be. Depends on God's grace. Not our worthiness.

– Not earned. Good works do not get it.

– No one is left out. Willie or us.

– This love gives us worth. We matter!

– Can reject it, but it keeps coming.

– Love is inclusive.

– We are loved. Can celebrate that today.

– "Jesus loves me, this I know."

C. Brainstorming Illustrations

I then spend some time thinking about illustrative material that would clearly picture the idea of the love of Jesus for all. I go through my own personal experiences and try to recall those moments when the love of God came to me. I always try to remember when the sermon took life for me. When did I first discover God's love? And how have I experienced it since? How have I seen it at work in the lives of others? Some images come to mind:

– Mother showing me love.

– Mary, alone and orphaned. Taken in by Smiths.

– Night in Virginia mountains, overwhelmed by a sense of God's love and presence.

After thinking about my personal stories, I then think about the stories of others. Are there some illustrations that others told that would be better in this sermon? This is when I go to those illustration cards that I had put into a pile on the desk. I go through them again, culling out the ones that I feel have good possibilities for this sermon. Any illustration that has potential, I put aside for further examination. Some came to the forefront.

– Story of the hunting dog

– The broken marriage that was healed

– Minister's daughter and school report

– Winston Churchill story

– WW II – Jim going for his friend in no-man's land

I will only use one of these illustrations. As I think about the point and start putting it together, usually the illustration that fits best, personal or otherwise, emerges. For now, I have several picture possibilities.

After I have brainstormed the point, I will put it aside for a time. I might make some hospital visits, eat lunch, play tennis. I want the ideas I have gathered to "simmer" for a while. I brood over them when I get the chance. Usually, the stronger ideas begin to "take root" in my thinking. So after a bit, I will then go back and move to the next step.

2. **Organizing the Ideas into an Image Outline.** The time of decision has come. How will I go about developing this first major section? The time has come to pick and choose. So I take out the paper and study it again. Through the brooding time, the idea has sharpened in my mind. So I will make an outline. I will seek to keep in mind the explanation, application, and illustration of the idea. Using the formula, I organize the point.

IDEA	PICTURE	IMAGE
1. Jesus stood up for the the woman when no one else would.	Text	Text

Note: Since I have the text down into a story that is happening again, all I need to do is to tell the story, emphasizing the places where the idea of love emerged. I do not need to put down many sentences. All I need to do is remember the story, see it in my head, and then describe it. So in the outline, all I need to put down is the word "text." That is enough to remind me of the biblical story.

2. Hear it, but do not believe it.	Love heard in a church	Disbelief
3. Feel we do not deserve it.	Woman felt unworthy	Woman
4. Try to earn it	Man, active in church	Churchworker
5. Can't be earned or deserved	Love ours already	Are loved
6. Illustration: daughter	Daughter	Daughter

Note: I do not have to put down many words here. This is a story that I let re-happen in my mind. Once I see it, I just retell it. One word should lead me into the story.

7. Love never stops	Love keeps coming for us all	Unstoppable

So the result of all that work is seven brief sentences. The sentences lead me into pictures which describe the idea. I then have gotten the pictures down into simple image words. If I remember those words, I should remember the pictures which I will describe to the people. When I do that, they will get the idea I wanted to communicate. Even if I felt I could not preach this sermon without notes, all I need to take into the pulpit is an outline of just the image words (or key words). So the outline for the first point would be:

Text
Disbelief
Woman
Churchworker
Are loved
Daughter
Love unstoppable

However, I feel that we will be able to learn these image words. If we learn them, then we can throw away the notes. We will need them no more. We have worked hard, wrestling with the text until it yielded the truth we felt needed to be preached. We have focused that idea into a thesis and objective. We have plotted the way we wanted to develop that truth clearly. We have spent time picturing the truth of the text coming to life and happening again. We have pictured that truth walking among the people, both as a problem and a solution. We have pictured possible illustrations – personal ones or from others – that could help us communicate that truth. We have brainstormed the idea, mulled over it, and finally organized it. After all of that work, I feel the sermon should be beginning to "take us over." We are becoming very familiar with it, so much so that we are getting to the place where we will not need notes to preach it. And even yet, there are some more steps we will take to help us absorb the sermon. (The next chapter) Proper preparation will help in preaching without notes.

3. **The Point Illustrated.** To help understand how this point was preached, I want to share with you the sermon text. I am jumping the gun in that I wrote the sermon out after I did the outline. I will

give some helps on how to do that in the next chapter. But I want you to see how the image outline can be developed and become the point. I will simply use the image word(s) and then describe what I said.

"Text"

A woman was caught in the act of adultery. No doubt about that. The Law of Moses said that when that happened, both the woman and the man (who seems to be missing here) were to be stoned to death. These religious leaders were ready to carry out that sentence. They had the stones in their hands. But they made a mistake. They brought her to Jesus and asked Him, "What should we do with her?"

Now notice. Nobody seemed to reach out to this woman. No one seemed to try to understand why she did what she did. Not one of the religious leaders seemed to have any compassion for her. In fact, the only reason they brought her to Jesus was so they might trick Him into making some mistake, going against the Law or against them. If He did that, then they could "get" Him. This woman was nothing but a pawn in their hands, a "thing" to be used at their desire. They did not care about her.

To their question, Jesus said nothing, just bent down and wrote something on the ground. They grew impatient. "Come on, man, what do you want us to do with her?" Finally, Jesus rose, looked at them and said, "Let the one who has no sin throw the first stone." And no one could! Instead, the stones dropped to the ground as one by one, they shuffled off.

Do you see what Jesus is doing here? He is standing up for this woman. He is defending her, watching out for her, caring for her. The religious leaders did not care, but Jesus did! This woman mattered to Him. It was for people like her that He had come in the first place. She mattered! No one else cared about her, but Jesus did!

"Disbelief"

Now we have heard all about that. We know that Jesus loves us. We talk about it all the time in church. We sing about it. We know that! But do we truly believe it? I am not too sure we do. As I have moved among people, I am coming to believe that we find God's love hard to accept. It seems too good to be true. Do you believe it? Do you really believe that God loves you?

"Woman"

I talked to a woman who had not lived too fine a life. She said to me that she was sure God could not love her. "After some of the things I've done, there is no way God could love me. I don't deserve the love of God." And she was right! None of us does. But she misunderstood that love. God's love for us does not depend on our deserving it. It depends on the grace of God that wants to give it, no matter what.

"Churchworker"

Or here was the man who was an active churchworker. Every time the doors of the church were open, he was there. Sunday morning, Sunday night, Wednesday night prayer service. If there was a committee that needed him, he was ready and willing to serve. If anything needed to be done, he stood up to do it. Someone asked him once, "Why do you do so much for the church? You are always there, giving so much of your time. Why?" And he answered, "Because I want to keep on the right side of God."

Do you hear what he was saying? He thought that if he kept doing good works for God, then somehow he would keep God loving him. But he was wrong! He was wrong because no matter how many good works he did, he could never earn the love of God. The reason? He already had it!

"Are loved"

This is the amazing truth of the gospel. We do not deserve the love of God – but no matter! It still comes to us. We can not earn the love of God – but no matter! It is already ours for the believing, for the trusting. No matter who we are and what we have done, here is the good news – for Willie, for you, for me. We are loved! Do you hear that? Do you believe that?

"Daughter"

A minister told of the time his daughter came to him in his office with a strange paper. On two sheets of paper were written 100 times the words, "I will not talk in school." As she showed him the paper, he looked at her face and noticed how pale she was. She had been hiding from him all day. He looked at her and said, "Sarah, how long have you carried this paper around with you?" She said, "For two days, and I have to get your signature." He said, "Why didn't you bring it to me sooner?" She said, "I was afraid of you." "What could you have been afraid of?" "I can't really tell you," she said. He persisted. "Were you afraid that I would beat you?" "Of course not." "Afraid that I would scold you?" "No." "Afraid that I would preach to you?" He then said, "Sarah, let me tell you something. If you were so bad that your picture was on the front page of all the newspapers as the epitome of everything we should not be, I would not love you any less. Conversely, if your picture was on the front page of every newspaper as a model of what everyone should be, I would not love you any more. Do you understand that?" She looked at him and said, "You see, that's what I was afraid of, Dad. You always tell me things that don't make any sense."[5]

"Unstoppable"

And it doesn't make any sense, does it? Here comes the love of God in Jesus, and no matter what we do in response to it – ignore it, reject it, laugh at it, put it on a cross and crucify it – there is one thing we can never do to it. We can never stop it! Here it comes – to Willie, to you, to me. No matter what we have been or done, it comes and puts its arms around us and says, "We are loved!" No one else will love us like that, but Jesus will. Do you believe it? Want it? Trust it?

Throughout this first point, I tried to think in pictures – through the story of the text, in the application, with the illustration. I tried to weave together the explanation, application, and illustration. The hope of the point was to help them see that we are all loved, no matter what! Hoping to have made that point, I tried not to "overkill it." Once I felt it was clear, I moved on to the next section, the one on forgiveness.

I hope you are getting a "feel" for the way the process works. Study the scripture, focus the idea, picture it, and image outline it. Having outlined the images, describe the pictures they present.

At the risk of overkill, I will quickly take you through the way I developed the second point, the one that said: Jesus is special because He will forgive you when no one else will.

1. **Brainstorming**

Explanation

    – All the religious leaders left.

    – No one to condemn.

    – Words of Jesus, "Neither do I condemn you."

    – She did not ask for it, but got it.

    – Forgiveness, even for adultery.

Application

    – Hear about it all the time.

    – Do not really believe this either.

    – Can not forgive each other.

    – Many people punishing themselves for mistakes committed long ago. Why can't they let them go?

    – Believe God forgives? Not really – not *our* sin!

    – Jesus said, "7 times 70."

Solution

    – God sent Jesus to die for our sins.

    – God is serious about forgiveness.

    – Jesus took away our sin.

    – Forgiveness for all sins — past, present, future.

    – Must not make a mockery of the cross.

    – God more interested in what we will become than in what we have been.

    – No matter what we have done, forgiveness is available – for Willie and for us.

Illustrations
Personal
      – Criticized over trumpet solo, hard to forgive.
      – Forgiveness from dad when I did not mow the lawn.
Others
      – Man went and helped those who had mugged him.
      – Bishop's sin.
      – Corrie ten Boom – forgiveness for guard.
      – Woman whose son was killed. "God says to forgive."

2. Organization into Image Outline

IDEA	PICTURE	IMAGE
1. Jesus forgave the woman	Text	Text
2. We do not believe forgiveness real	People can not forgive themselves	Unbelievable
3. God forgives through Christ.	Cross event	Cross
4. Forgiveness for all sins	Future is most important	Clean slate
5. Illustration: Bishop's sin	Bishop	Bishop
6. Forgiveness is the gospel!	Forgiven!	Forgiven!

3. The Point Developed

"Text"

    Jesus turns to the woman. "Where are the ones who accuse you?" "They are all gone," she replied. "Neither do I condemn thee." Did you hear that? Here is a woman guilty of the terrible sin of adultery and here is Jesus saying to her, "Forgiven!" They would not forgive her. No one would – except for Jesus. He did!

"Unbelievable"

    Jesus forgives us of our sins. We know that, too. We talk about it, sing about it, in our prayers we always ask for "the forgiveness of our sins." We know all about it – but do we believe it is true? Again, I am not so sure. This is another idea that seems to be too good to be true. Let me ask you: do you feel God will forgive you of your sin?

I have talked to many through the years who tell the same old story. They committed some terrible sins in the past and they are still plagued by guilt because of them. That guilt robs them of sleep at night. "Have you asked God to forgive you?" I ask. "Oh, yes," they say. "But we just feel God can't forgive us for what we've done."

There you have it. Unbelief! Feeling that forgiveness may be for others, but not for them. Do you ever feel like that? Your sin is so terrible that not even God can forgive it?

"Cross"

But if there is one thing I am sure God was serious about, it was the forgiveness of sin. So serious was God that Jesus was sent to die on the cross for them. The death of Christ was not too high a price for God to pay to bring us forgiveness. Forgiveness is real! Whenever we don't think it is, we make a mockery of that cross. God was serious. Forgiveness is available for us if we want it.

"Clean Slate"

Why is it that some of us are still punishing ourselves for sins that God has long since forgiven? We do not have to punish ourselves. Don't we see? God is more concerned about what we will become than in what we have done. No matter what we have done, no matter how terrible it might have been, in Christ God says, "O.K. Let's forget about that and move on. Let's leave the mistakes behind and live for Me now." And God said that to you, to me, to Willie, and all the Willies of the world. No one else may care to forgive, but Jesus will!

"Bishop"

One of my Catholic friends told me a story that was making the rounds among them. A certain nun had a vision of Christ; Christ appeared to her. The Bishop had to go and "check out" the validity of that vision. "So Christ

91

appeared to you?" he asked. "Yes," she answered. "And not only that, Christ told me that He was going to come and visit me again." The Bishop had an idea. He told her, "Before I became a Bishop, I committed a terrible sin. The only one who would know what it was besides me would be Christ. If He comes to visit you again, ask Him what was the Bishop's terrible sin." "I'll do that," she said. The Bishop left, thinking he had taken care of that matter.

However, a few months later, the nun called and wanted to see the Bishop. Christ had appeared to her again. Nervously, the Bishop drove down to see her. "So Christ appeared to you again?" "Yes." "Well, did you remember to ask Him that question I wanted you to ask?" "Oh, yes. You wanted me to ask Him what your terrible sin was." "Did you?" "Yes, I did." Now quite nervously, the Bishop asked, "What did Jesus say?" And the nun replied, "Jesus said that He had forgotten."

"Forgiven!"

Did you hear that? That is the gospel! For you, for me, for Willie. God is more concerned about what we will become than in punishing us for our past sins. Listen! Forgiveness is real! No one else may forgive us, but we can bet our lives that Jesus will! (For the full text of this sermon, see the Appendix)

IMAGING THE CONCLUSION

The final piece of the puzzle is ending the sermon in the right way. The conclusion is the place where we seek to "drive home" the specific objective for the sermon. What do we want them to do because of it? What decision do we hope they make?

A few guidelines might be helpful:

1. **Be brief.** Do not prolong the conclusion. We are to bring the sermon to an end quickly. It is the "back porch" of the sermon. It is the way out of the house. We do not linger on that porch. By the time we get to the conclusion, the sermon idea has hopefully been developed. If not, it is too late to try to redo it.

2. **Avoid "denoting" words.** By that, I mean do not tell them such phrases as "in conclusion," "I conclude," or "finally." These words try to denote the fact that we have arrived at the end. Let's leave them out. I have heard too many say, "let me conclude," and we gave them our permission, but they did not do it! They just went on and on. May we beware of making promises that we will not keep! A conclusion concludes. We do not have to tell them the sermon is over. If done well, they will discover that.

3. **Major on application.** Do not get too bogged down in the text explanation here. The conclusion brings the sermon into the *now*. If the truth takes hold of their lives now, what will happen? Picture the sermon objective coming to life among them.

4. **Use illustrations that illustrate the whole sermon idea.** An illustration can be a powerful way to end a sermon if it is the right one. Such an illustration must not illustrate only the last point, but the total sermon idea. If we can find the right illustration, it can leave the people with a great picture to remember. Sometimes it can "save" a sermon that is going nowhere. A student once preached a sermon on how God's suffering was meaningful, but I was confused by what was meant by that. All the way through the sermon, I was lost. Then at the end, he told of the time when he was about to give up – his faith, his work, even his life! But at that moment, he remembered how Christ had suffered for him and that gave him the hope to go on. If Christ cared that much for him, to suffer that much, then surely Christ understood his pain. So he kept on! When the student told that story, the sermon came together for me. I understood! And even now, I still remember the story. That is the power of a well-chosen illustration.

5. **Bring the people to a point of decision.** As I have mentioned before, when we preach we just do not try to pass the time of day. We are there to persuade – to seek to lead people into a relationship with God that leads to a committed discipleship. It is our prayer that the sermon will make a life-changing, life-affirming difference in their lives. We want something to happen because of the sermon.

They must make that decision. We cannot make it for them. But we must make sure they know they have a decision to make. We must clearly present the choices. As I think of this, I am reminded of a minister who used to ask us every Tuesday at the ministers' meeting, "How many decisions did you have Sunday?" He was looking for numbers, how many "walked the aisle." That would get under my skin. Finally, I decided how to answer him. One Tuesday, when he asked how many decisions I had on Sunday, I said, "450." His eyes popped wide open, his jaw dropped to his chest. "What do you mean?" he asked. "Well," I said, "I preached the Word of God and in response to that, some said, 'yes,' some said, 'no,' and some said, 'I'll think about it.' But everyone made a decision, as they must do whenever the Word of God is preached." (See Acts 17:32-24) He never asked me that question again.

That story reminds me that there is always the temptation on our part to try to manipulate people, to make their decisions for them. We cannot – and must not – do that! They must decide for themselves. We are to paint the positive picture of the gospel, the good news. We must always seek to leave people with hope, never sending them home on a "flat tire." The decision, however, is totally theirs. Our struggle is to make that decision clear – and then trust the Holy Spirit to do the convicting and the leading toward the proper choices.

Like the rest of the sermon, brainstorm the best way to end, then put it into an image outline. For the sermon on Willie, which had an evangelistic objective, the outline ended up like this:

IDEA	PICTURE	IMAGE
1. Recess ended, Willie left	Willie	Willie
2. Summary of what I had said	Summary	Summary
3. Willie's fate	Fate	Fate
4. Do we believe it?	Decision	Decision

The conclusion, written out, went like this:
"Willie"

> Well, the bell rang and recess was over. It was time to go. Willie thanked me and said he would think about what I had said.

94

"Summary"

That was what I told him that day – and what I have been trying to tell others ever since. Willie, Jesus is special because He will love you when no one else will. You matter to Him. You are special. And Jesus will forgive you when no one else will. Willie, whatever you have done can be left behind. Jesus is more interested in today than yesterday. And if you trust this Jesus, He will help you to become more than you have ever dreamed. The possibilities are unlimited for your future if you let Jesus help you live it. Life can become an exciting adventure.

"Fate"

I asked Willie several times after that, "Have you thought about what we talked about?" He always said, "I'm still thinking about it." Well, school ended and I went a thousand miles away to seminary and lost touch with Willie. A few years ago, I found out what happened to him. Willie had dropped out of school, joined the armed forces, went to a place called Vietnam. And there – Willie died!

"Decision"

When I heard that, I hoped in my soul that what I told Willie that day in that schoolyard, somehow he believed. And I hope that you do. The word for Willie is a word for every one of us. There is no one who will love us, forgive us, believe in us like Jesus. Do you believe that? Will you trust Him to do that for you?

Never underestimate the importance of the conclusion. Give deep thought to it. Lead the sermon to its proper climax. Always have that specific objective in mind as we write it. Lead the people to the point of decision, and then trust them to the care of the Holy Spirit.

RECAP

This chapter has focused on the development of an image outline, seeking to get the sermon into a set of images that could be painted like a mural on a wall. If we see the images, we can recall the sermon.

There is an important formula to help us accomplish that: IDEA to PICTURE to IMAGE. What is the idea we want to communicate? What does that idea look like? Can we "take" a picture of it and get it into our minds? Then from that picture, we select a word or two that will help us image the picture, making it easier for us to remember. So then the formula will reverse itself. IMAGE to PICTURE to IDEA. If we remember the image, we then recall the picture. We describe the picture we have in our minds to others, and when we do that, they will understand the sermon idea.

Sounds simple enough, doesn't it? To preach without notes, what we do is learn the images. There are some other steps we can take to help us do that. To these, I now turn.

---

1. Warren W. Wiersbe, *Preaching and Teaching With Imagination* (Wheaton, Illinois: Victor Books, 1994), 42.

2. *Ibid.*, 43.

3. Robert Hughes, "The Controlling Image: One Key to Sermon Unity," *Academy Accents* (newsletter of the Academy of Preachers), Winter, 1991, 2.

4. For a comprehensive study of biblical metaphors, see Wiersbe, *op. cit.*, 89-198.

5. David H. C. Read, sermon, *National Radio Pulpit*, July-August-September, 1972, 15-16.

Chapter Five

Practice Run: Absorbing The Sermon

One of the few things I remember about my science classes was a simple experiment. (If you saw my grades in science, you would be amazed that I can remember anything about it.) In it, the teacher dropped one drop of blue dye into a glass of water. We watched, and in an instant, that drop of blue dye was totally absorbed by the water. It was gone, missing, disappeared. But then the teacher put another drop in, then another, and another, and – presto! Soon the water in the glass had turned completely blue. It had "taken over" the water and transformed it.

I have thought of that experiment as an example of what I am trying to do with my sermon. I liken myself to that glass of water and the blue dye to the sermon. What I hope will happen is that the sermon will eventually "take me over," capturing me with its truth. For that to happen, I need to do what is necessary to get it "inside" of me. I have been working hard to get the sermon into a "preachable" form. I have focused it, pictured it, gotten it down into an image outline that could be put down on paper. What I do not want to do is to leave the sermon "out there" on a piece of paper. I want to bring it inside of me, so I will feel it, breathe it, be absorbed by it.

How do I get it inside of me so that it transforms me, becomes a part of me? It is like putting in drop after drop of blue dye into the water. One drop will not do. I have to take some intentional steps to get the sermon inside of me. I feel these steps are two: writing the sermon and practicing the sermon. These two activities, if done seriously, can help us absorb the sermon, or let the sermon absorb us.

WRITING THE SERMON

Once in a while in class, I come across a student who seems to boast proudly, "I've never written a sermon in my life." All I can say is, "Well, you will at least write three of them." They do not particularly seem too happy about that. But my guess is that if I talked to the people to whom they preached, I would probably hear the criticism that they say the same things over again, or that they are guilty of "rambling" all over the place. This usually happens if sermons are not thought through. Writing can help us do that.

Now writing does take time. Sometimes it is easy to want to save time and just get the sermon into an outline and "wing it" from there. There is no doubt that if we have gone through the preparation process and gotten a good image outline, that we may be able to "wing it" much more easily. As we remember the images, we can just tell about the pictures they provoke. We can describe what we see and we surely do not need notes for that, do we?

Toward an Oral Style

There are many who would agree with that. A great deal of emphasis is being placed today on preparing the sermon in an oral style. Sermons are not to be written, they are to be spoken. There is a tremendous difference between a sermon prepared to be read and one prepared to be spoken. I have read many a sermon that looked good on paper, but when it was delivered, crashed like a ton of bricks. The reason: it was not delivered in an oral style. What are some of the differences between a written and oral style?

1. **Oral style is for the moment.** If a person is reading a sermon and does not quite understand a part of it, one can go back and re-read it and think about it again. If necessary, one can read it over several times until it makes sense. One can take all the time needed to do that.

But when the sermon is spoken, the idea must be clear and understood in that moment. People can not go back and re-read it. In speaking, we get that one chance to get the idea across. If we do not do it then, it usually means the hearer will be lost the rest of the way through the sermon. We must develop language that is clear, descriptive, picturesque, that can give them a good picture immediately, one that they can carry with them in understanding the message.

2. **Oral style must continuously recapture attention.** In reading, if the concentration is broken, it can be recaptured. If a baby cries, or the phone rings, or it is time for supper – no problem. Just go back and pick up where you left off. Review if necessary, but it is not that hard to get back on track.

In hearing a sermon, concentration can be easily disturbed. A crying child, a dropped hymn book, a fly buzzing around somebody's head, the sound of a siren as the ambulance whizzes by outside – such things can disrupt the concentration people need to hear a sermon. After the momentary disturbance is over, they can not go back and start all over again. It is too late for that. How can they get back on track? This is where oral style comes in. It must seek continuously to recapture their attention. This can be done by repetition, especially repeating the main idea or ideas at several intervals. Illustrative material is excellent in recapturing attention gone astray. It is scary sometimes how quiet it gets when we start telling a compelling story. Everyone is listening! Every now and then, it might be good to summarize in a sentence or two what we have said, so that those who have gotten lost for a while might find their way back into the sermon.

Oral style needs to use material that not only will be interest-catching, but will help keep the sermon idea alive.

3. **Oral style is more personal.** Written style is often impersonal. A sermon that is published in a book is for "whom it may concern." It has a more formal style. When I published some of my sermons in written form for the people in the church, I would record them on a dictaphone when I preached. My secretary would then type it out for me to read. I would "edit" it so that it would read well. I would try to be less personal, less informal in style. Phrases that would be easily understood when spoken had to be re-written for the eye. I always felt like the printed sermons lost some of their life. Gone was the power of my personality or the power of the moment when preacher and people met in dialogue.

Gordon Clinard, as I mentioned elsewhere, made a statement that has stuck to me like glue. He said, "Preaching is conversation he pulpit." When we stand in the pulpit to preach, what do is to carry on a conversation with one person. If 500 overhear that conversation, well and good. But I am not trying to preach to 500, but to have a conversation with only one.

I have found that idea has freed me in delivery. I am daily carrying on conversations with others about what I see and know and think. I usually do not have a problem with that. You talk with people, dialogue with them, and you communicate naturally through that process. Lift it up to the pulpit! Be that personal and informal. Oral style does not worry so much about "split infinitives" or "dangling participles." Precise and correct grammar is not as important as communicating with others. Now before English teachers start a crusade to ban me from life (and my mother was an English teacher), I am *not* calling for sloppiness in the use of language. We still have to make sense and be understood. Good use of the English language will enable us to do that. What I am calling for is a style that is not so stiff and formal, but personal and conversational. In preaching, we are not speaking to the world in general, but to a person in particular. Have a conversation with him. Imagine a dialogue with him. Talk "back and forth" with him in your mind. That is essential to the development of an oral style. Remember, it is not, "I want to speak a word to Christians today." It is, "I want to speak a word to you."

4. **Oral style is less complex.** Written style is often able to take us through long, involved and complex arguments. We can take our time as we read to figure out these ideas, step by step. We do not have that time in hearing a sermon. Ideas need to be presented in a clear, direct, straight-forward way. I have heard sermons that I felt were created to confuse us. They were almost impossible to follow. When all was said and done, we looked at each other and shook our heads. We did not understand what we had heard.

I hope people will not shake their heads in confusion after our sermons. That is what I hope the cover page will help us do – preach sermons that are direct and clear in idea and purpose. Especially in preaching without notes, complex ideas are difficult to recall. So again, in preaching we are seeking to communicate one idea – and one idea only. We do not want it to be a secret. Develop an oral style that will get to the point, emphasize it, and make it clear.

5. **Oral style can communicate emotions more easily.** Sometimes, written sermons can be very moving, stirring the emotions. But more often, they are less so. Emotions are not all that easy to convey through the printed word. In reading scripture, this is one of the frustrations we sometimes have. How did Jesus say that, we wonder? Did He use a gentle voice, an angry one, a stern one? What feeling was put into the words spoken? It is not easy to know. We have to use our imaginations often to put in the feelings of the people in the stories we read.

Not so in oral style. The spoken word can convey passion and emotions much more easily. As the people listen to us, they will catch how we feel. If we talk about love, do they feel it from us? If we are angry about a situation, do they feel our anger? If we are dealing with the hurts of others, do they feel our pain for them? If we are excited about some good news we have, do they sense how joyful we are? This is a major plus of oral style. When we speak, we can display the emotion we want to convey. Oral language "feels." Hopefully, people will not wonder what they are to feel about the idea or truth shared.

A note of caution: This is one reason I want to try to get the sermon inside of us, to absorb it. If we can, then we will "feel" it, understand the moods and emotions of it. Such emotions must be honest and "in sync" with the material. We do not manufacture the emotion. If the material deals with love, hopefully that emotion will flow out from us naturally. And to be "in sync" means that when we talk about love, we do not do so in a hateful manner. Have you ever heard someone talk about how God loves us but glowers at us while talking? Likewise, if it is painful material, we do not laugh or smile. If it is joyful, we do not talk like we are at a funeral. Let the emotion flow naturally from the kind of material presented. If we do that, sermons can be very moving and touch the honest emotions of the people.

An Oral Manuscript

To develop that oral style, many homileticians are emphasizing the oral presentation of the sermon. Speaking out loud is preferred to writing it down. Fred Craddock, who was instrumental in arousing interest in inductive preaching, wrote that preaching style would be improved greatly by "preparing orally from the outset."[1] Eugene Lowry, a strong proponent of narrative preaching, says it more simply. "Prepare sermons out loud."[2] Clyde Fant, another of my preaching mentors, has written in his book, *Preaching for Today*, about an "oral manuscript."[3] This manuscript is prepared in several stages.

1. **Initial study.** This involves the study of the text which leads to a tentative plan for the sermon. This work has to be done for every sermon. This stage is "a matter of thought, but beyond this early stage it should be a matter of speech. The tentative direction of the sermon that thought has suggested should be made definite through speaking."[4]

2. **The rough oral draft.** Fant suggests that we put each of the major movements (or signposts) of the theme on a separate sheet of paper. We should then preach aloud on each of them as long as ideas present themselves. Keep a pen in hand and pause in speaking only long enough to write down key phrases and ideas that emerge. This exercise is similar to the brainstorming procedures I presented earlier.

Fant notes that "this state corresponds exactly with the writing of the rough draft of the manuscript – except that it is being done in the medium that will eventually be used."[5] Speaking saves time, Fant contends, because we speak usually five to ten times faster than we write.

After we are finished with the major movements of the sermon, we repeat the same process for the introduction and the conclusion.

3. **The final oral manuscript.** After the rough draft has been done, we should next re-examine the notes. Re-arrange the key sentences or movements into the order that seems to be called for by the speaking process. Select the ideas that we find useful and eliminate those that aren't. Revise the notes as needed. Once that is done, we preach it out loud again. This will be the final draft of

the oral manuscript. Continue to revise and edit as needed. But remember, all of this work is being done in the medium in which the sermon will be presented.

4. **The sermon brief.** Fant presents the idea of the sermon brief – not an outline or a manuscript – but a brief. It is a condensation of the basic truths of the sermon. Such a sermon brief would look like this:

Sermon Brief

Introduction
3-5
sentences

_____
_____.
_____.

_____
_____ .

Basic Directional Sentence (Division)

_____
_____.

6-10
sentences

_____ Key sentences, each
_____ introducing its own
_____. thought block of
discussion. (Exploring
_____. the biblical material
_____. and the contemporary
situation; presenting
_____ pictorial,
_____. illustrative material, etc.)

Basic Directional Sentence (Division)
(etc.)

_____.

Conclusion _____
3-5   _____.
sentences

            _____
            _____.[6]

Fant has listed several advantages for this approach.
A.   The sermon has produced the instrument rather than the instrument producing the sermon, as is the case with the manuscript.
B.   It is truer to the nature of conversation. It will lend itself to better conversational delivery.
C.   It does not tie the preacher to the wording of a manuscript. It allows that freedom of creation and spontaneity of response that are essential if preaching is to be an event in the worship service. It offers up the possibility of having a true dialogue with the people.
D.   The sermon brief does give focus and direction to the sermon. It will serve to keep the preacher "on track."
E.   The oral process of preparation results in an oral product for the oral medium of preaching.[7]

I commend Fant's approach to us. It can be a tremendous aid to our sermon preparation. I would submit that his idea of a sermon brief I would call an "image outline." Both methods call for a brainstorming of the ideas. I would encourage speaking out loud as we brainstorm. The organization of the sermon into key transitional sentences is what I have sought to do under the section of "idea" in the image outline. Where I have expanded on Fant's approach is with the use of the sections "picture" and "image." I would like the brief to be further condensed from the key sentences, eventually being captured in an image of a word or two. I feel this process would make the sermon easier to remember. I think all of the advantages Fant lists for his sermon brief will be the same for my image outline.

I am in debt to Fant for his work in the area of preaching without notes. Much of my system is an outgrowth of the ideas I learned under his teaching. His method went a long way in helping me develop my note-free preaching. The system I have developed simply carries the process a bit further. From my experience, I feel an image outline further clarifies the sermon material and the sermon direction. It also provides an easier tool for remembering the sermon.

Oral preparation is good. Speaking a sermon out loud, brainstorming it out loud, can unleash creative thoughts we never thought we had. Many times when I was trying to develop a sermon, I got stuck. The ideas did not flow – or even come. When that happened, I would often go into the sanctuary, shut the doors so no one would hear, go and stand in the pulpit and start preaching and talking out loud. I would just state the idea and say anything that came to mind. Amazingly, ideas started coming to the surface. I would jot them down and the sermon would begin to form.

I have always tried to figure out why that happened. I do feel that we think better on our feet than on our seat. When we preach, we are standing, so maybe standing puts us at ease and enables us to think more easily. Sometimes I feel the ideas flow because the pulpit is "where the action is." Somehow, being there sets the ideas loose. I do not really know why it happens. I can just testify that it has happened for me. Maybe you can try it. The next time you get "stuck," go into the pulpit and start speaking out loud. See what happens.

Putting it Down

Even though there are tremendous advantages to preparing an oral manuscript, I am still one who believes that a sermon needs to be written down. This is done only after all the other steps have been taken. Writing is not the first thing we do to develop the sermon. It is one of the last steps we take.

1. **Advantages**
   A. A theological rationale.

   > For me, preaching is a sacred matter. We stand to speak a word in behalf of God. We must be sure that we have brought our best effort to that moment. The discipline of writing can help us present the best developed sermon we can. It can prevent sloppiness.

B. It will help us avoid the false crutch of the "gift of gab."

One of the dangers for preachers is to fall into the belief that God has blessed us with the "gift of gab." We are always talking. People are always asking us questions, waiting to hear a word from us. So we learn to talk, to have ready answers available on the tips of our tongues. However, sometimes I feel that our mouths operate when our minds do not. We think we are saying something profound and deep when it is shallow and worthless. We just talk without much thinking.

I have had students tell me that they just get an outline of the sermon and take that into the pulpit with them. That is all they need. They see key words and then they will be able to talk about that. They have not thought too much about what they are going to say, but they are confident "something will come to them." As one said, "I always think of something to say."

The danger in that is that we often get into bad habits doing it. We develop "pet phrases" that we use over and over again. We often use the verbal pause – the "uh" – as we are trying to come up with something to say. Or we end up saying the "same old things" repeatedly. We must beware of that, of speaking "off the cuff." I talked to a church member who said about her extemporaneous-speaking preacher, "He just says the same thing over and over again in the same old way with the same old words."

We do not want that said about us. Writing will help us avoid our dependence upon the gift of gab.

C. Writing will help us think through the sermon idea.

As we write the sermon from beginning to end, we can get a good sense of how the sermon flows. Does it make sense? Does it move logically from one step to the next? Does it move to a good climax? Does it fit together as a whole?

A sermon must make sense. Writing helps us to think it through, to see that it does make sense. Writing forces us to think through how we are going to speak the sermon.

Therefore, we can get a better "handle" on the total thrust of it. It can be better grasped by our minds. If we have thought it through and it makes sense, it should be easier to remember.

D. Writing helps to develop our own unique style.

How can we best express the idea? What words and phrases can be used? What pictures would be best to describe it? How I would say it is not the way that you might choose to say it. Each of us has our own unique way of speaking the truth. Writing aids the development of that unique style. How will *you* say it?

Writing helps polish up our style. As we write, we are thinking about how we will say what we want. When we put down the words, that is our style. As we write, we might think of new and creative ways to say what we want. Writing can turn loose our imaginations and allow us to see new ways to communicate. If we do not write, we may fall into that habit of saying the same old things in the same old ways. Writing can keep us fresh and creative, finding new ways to unwrap God's truth.

E. Writing will help us absorb the sermon.

Writing is one discipline that can help get the sermon "out there" into us. As we think it through, when we put down the words, we are subconsciously learning the sermon. The memory is amazing. As we work through the process of sermon development, we are learning more of the sermon than we think. All that we do makes an impression on our memories. I have discovered that after I have gone through the sermon preparation process presented here, I usually will remember eighty percent of the sermon without any difficulty. Writing is a key to that, helping me to absorb what I have been thinking about. It might be an interesting exercise for you to try. After you write out the sermon, put away that manuscript and start preaching out loud what you can remember. If you forget something, don't worry about it. Go on to the next thought you remember. You might be surprised at how much of the sermon you already know. Writing helps us absorb the sermon.

F.   Writing keeps the sermon available for future use.

If we ever want to preach the sermon again – and we sometimes do that – we will have the full manuscript available. If the sermon was just kept in an outline form, because of the passing of time, we might not remember all the ideas and images that we used. Writing the sermon enables us to keep the sermon and recall it.

If we do preach the sermon again, we should always go over it carefully, revising it for the new place and occasion. We may need to change some ideas or illustrations or images. We definitely need to absorb it again, seeking to make it a part of us. We need to re-live the process that brought the sermon to life. We need to see the pictures happening again, the text coming alive anew, the illustrations actually taking place. In a way, we are not to "warm up" the stew, we are to "re-cook" it. The sermon manuscript can serve as a basis for this new meal.

There may be other advantages for writing out the sermon. But some of you might be objecting. You can not do that. It will take too much time. It can not be done. All I can say to that is for seventeen years, I preached two different sermons each Sunday and wrote out both of them. It takes discipline, but it can be done. If we believe in the importance of preaching, we will make the effort to see if we can do it. And it will not take as much time as you might think. Why not?

2. **Getting the Picture**

Remember what we did to get our image outline? We first got an idea. Then we pictured that idea, tried to imagine what it would look like. We then condensed that picture into an image of a word or two. The hope is that when we remember the image, it will help us remember the picture. When we describe the picture we have in our minds to others, then the sermon idea will be understood.

When we write the sermon, what we seek to write are the "pictures" we have developed in our minds. Recall the illustrations and then simply write down how we will describe them to the people. We write down what we see. Do not spend a great deal of time on precise word choice or sentence structure. Just write down the words that come as we describe the pictures that appear in our minds.

When we do this, we will write it as we will say it. Our writing will be in an oral style. It will be writing for the ear. Our manuscript will not be one that will make for good reading, but it will be one that will make for good speaking.

When we write down the pictures we see, we will be using descriptive language, language that will help others to see. The purpose of the words and phrases will be to enable the idea to be seen. When my children drew pictures of what they had seen but could not describe in words, I then was able to understand the idea. This is the same process. What did you see? In preaching, draw it for me by telling me about it. Then write down what you told me. This is what I am suggesting we do to write the sermon.

I have learned that when I do that – writing down the descriptions of the pictures – that the writing does not take too long. I have been thinking about these pictures for a long time. I have talked over them out loud and worked to get them into an image outline. I have gotten the pictures into key image words that summarize the pictures for me. All of that has not been in vain. It has helped the sermon grow in my memory. So when I write down the pictures, I am not creating something new to be put down on paper. I am simply recording what I have already developed through the preparation process. For me, writing the sermon down seldom took more than an hour or two.

Unbelievable! It seems so. But do not throw away the possibility yet! Follow the process through and see what happens. And remember this: the more you do it, the easier it will get. It is simply putting down on paper the "oral manuscript" we have been developing since step one of the sermon process.

Please understand this. Once we have written the sermon down into a manuscript, the manuscript is still our servant, not our master. It serves as a guideline for what we will say. It can be an aid to helping us absorb it. But we must not feel compelled to preach the sermon exactly as we have written it. We are not to be slaves to words. We are seeking to share the pictures and we may use different words to describe them each time we share them. Writing helps us think the descriptions through, but we will still have great freedom to use any words we feel communicate best in the moment of delivery. When the students preach in class, I require them to give me a full manuscript of the sermon. But I tell them that I do not expect them to go by it word for word – or even paragraph by paragraph. If they do, I know they have memorized the sermon. I do not want them to do that. I want them to absorb it, absorb the images and pictures and be so "in love" with them, that they will not have any difficulty telling me what they have seen. When they preach the sermon, I want them to see pictures which they describe to me, not words that they repeat.

Give it a try! Write the sermon pictures down. Do not worry about it being eloquent or striking or clever. Seek to be clear about what we see. Then describe it so that others can see it like we do.

THE PRACTICE RUNS

I am a firm believer in practicing the delivery of the sermon. It is an important step in absorbing the sermon.

A Rationale

To preach effectively, we need to develop the skills of the communication art. Since preaching is an oral activity, we need to "fine tune" our oral skills. We must also work to understand the proper body language that communicates best. To do that, practicing the delivery of a sermon is vital.

Imagine a singer scheduled to give a concert. Do you think she just shows up that night and sings away? Hardly! Before the concert, she spends hours and hours rehearsing for it, learning and practicing the songs, working on the vocal skills needed to sing them properly. During that time, she corrects mistakes, learns the best way to present the songs, gains confidence in her ability to sing them well. So when the concert comes, it is done well, mainly because of the practice that was done beforehand.

Likewise, a piano player would not present a piano recital without long hours of practice. I had a pianist tell me that he practiced at least eight hours a day for his concerts. When the day for the concert came, playing it was almost like second nature to him because of the many times he had practiced the music before. Concerts were fun for him, mainly because he had worked out the "bugs" during the rehearsing. A skilled performance was due to disciplined practice.

A sermon is created to be spoken, not just written. Sometimes a person is asked, "Are you ready for Sunday?" He says, "Yes, I just finished writing my sermon this afternoon." My contention is that once a sermon has been written, we are only halfway ready to preach. That other half is learning how to deliver the sermon effectively. If that study mentioned earlier is right (p. 12), and 93 percent of the effectiveness of a sermon depends upon factors other than content, we need to pay attention to those factors. Maybe we have heard a sermon that was full of good content and strong biblical truth, but it was delivered in such a way that people were bored to death. As good as the content was, it was not heard. Then you heard another preacher and his sermon was full of theological "fluff," saying nothing. But he delivered it in such a way that the people were impressed and awed by it. "What a great preacher he is!" Bad content, but good delivery!

The idea is for a sermon to have good content and to be delivered effectively. To have something worthwhile to say and to say it in a worthwhile way – that is our goal. We have spent a great deal of time in creating a good "product," full of moving pictures and images that will clearly share the truth. Now we must pay attention to the second part – saying it in a worthwhile manner.

Practicing a sermon will help us do that. For when we practice a sermon, we will be using all the factors that matter in delivery: the voice, the body movement, gestures, etc. If we concentrate on what we are doing with these factors, it can lead to our using them more meaningfully. For example, one of the hopes of preaching is that we will begin to listen to the sound of our own voice. What does it sound like? Are we stuck in a monotone pattern, not using the whole range of our voice, but only two or three "notes" of it?

Are we pronouncing our words correctly? Are we emphasizing important words with our voice? In practice, we can start paying attention to these questions, seeing if we can develop a sense of how our voice sounds.

The videotape is one of the best helps for preaching that has come along in recent years. Through it, we can see ourselves as others see us when we preach. Students usually have two reactions when they see themselves on the video for the first time. "It wasn't as bad as I thought it was going to be." They are usually surprised at how well they do look when delivering a sermon. The second reaction? "I didn't know I was doing that!" This refers to some habit they have when preaching, like scratching the nose, looking at the ceiling, swaying back and forth, putting their hands in their pockets, using too many "uhs," dropping the last sounds of a phrase, etc. The camera does not lie. Good communication is not noticed. The messenger does not get in the way of the message. If there is anything we do that gets in the way of good communication, we must try to eliminate it. Practice is the time to concentrate on overcoming these problems. The more we work to develop a smoother delivery, the better we will become.

Recently a student who had not done much preaching spoke in class. In the feedback time, the class was impressed with her delivery factors. It seemed to them as if she was an experienced preacher. They were surprised to learn how little she had preached. But she did well because she took seriously the practicing of the sermon. She worked on the elements that went into a good delivery. Like that singer or pianist, she worked to correct her mistakes, to learn how to best speak her sermon, and to seek to absorb it. When she preached it, she had no trouble remembering it. It was almost like "second nature" to her. Why was she so effective? I believe it was because of the preparation and practice put in beforehand. The old saying is that "practice makes perfect." Well, I do not think it will really help us preach a perfect sermon, but it certainly will help us preach a better one.

Do you practice your sermon? I would challenge you to try it for three months. Go into the sanctuary, lock all the doors so no one will think you have gone crazy, go up to the pulpit and "let her rip." Try to listen to yourself. Pay attention to how you speak the sermon, what you do with your hands and your body, how you feel when you speak the different parts of the message. I make a contract with my students to practice the sermon at least five times before they preach it. Try that! Remember – you will be practicing in the medium in which the sermon will be given. See if it makes a difference in your delivery. I really feel it will. Good preparation makes for a more confident delivery.

A Procedure

To learn to preach without notes, we need to take the sermon through some "practice runs." I would suggest the following procedure.

RUN ONE

Take into the pulpit the full written manuscript. Read it out loud. Seek to read it with expression and feeling. If there are sections that you feel that you already know, such as an illustration, go ahead and just tell that. Otherwise, read it just like you wrote it. Try to listen to yourself to see if you can hear how it sounds. The emphasis here is not on trying to remember the sermon, but going through it out loud.

RUN TWO

Put away the full manuscript and bring out the more extensive image outline. This is the one that contains the "idea-picture-image" columns. Place it on the pulpit and start preaching, using only the outline as your guide. You see the idea, then try to recall the picture and describe it out loud. If you come across a section that you can not remember, just move on to the next section, or to the next part you do remember. Go all the way through the sermon using only the image outline.

After you finish, bring out the full manuscript and compare it with what you did. Were there sections you left out? Were there pictures you forgot? If you did forget something, why did you? Is the material too hard to remember? Is it out of place? Try to figure out why you forgot what you did.

My guess is that you will be surprised at how much of the sermon you did remember. With the help of the full image outline, you probably did not forget too much.

All the while you are preaching, seek to listen to yourself. Pay some attention to what you are doing with your body, such as your hands. See if you are feeling comfortable with what you are doing.

RUN THREE

This time, only take into the pulpit an outline of just the image words, that last column in the image outline. Using these image words, start preaching the sermon. If you get stuck on one image and cannot remember what it signifies, plod on to the next one. Do not look at anything else. Just use the image words.

When you finish, pull out the image outline or the manuscript and see how you did. What did you forget? Maybe these are the sections you will need to concentrate on more seriously in order to remember the sermon. Again, I feel you will be surprised by how much material you do remember. All the preparation you have done is "burning" the sermon into your soul. Usually, I find that most students remember at least eighty percent of the sermon at this point. Often it is more than that.

RUN FOUR

This is the time to "launch out into the deep." Take no notes into the pulpit. Just start preaching the sermon and try to go all the way through it. If you forget, go on to the next thought you remember. Always keep in mind your road map, especially the signposts that mark the sermon's journey. If you think you are lost, remember them and let them get you back on the trail.

After you have made your way through, take out the outline and see how you did. What did you forget and why? Zero in on those sections, trying to understand them more clearly.

RUN FIVE AND BEYOND

Try it again without notes. See if it goes better this time. Usually by this time, the sermon is becoming a part of you. You are absorbing it. If you need to, run through it again. Begin to feel comfortable with it. Begin to gain the confidence that you do know the sermon and can preach it without notes. When you are just learning this process, you might need to practice it more than five times. As you gain more experience with it, five times will usually be enough.

Now these "practice runs" can be done all at once – or over a period of two or three days. Usually two to three hours of practice will begin to get the sermon inside of us. And all the while we are doing this practice, we are improving the physical skills needed to deliver sermons effectively.

Discoveries

During these practice runs, we might make some discoveries about our sermon.

1. **Some material does not sound right.** We may begin to hear what we are saying and sometimes, it may not sound too great. For example, clever phrases that looked good when we wrote them down may not sound good when we speak them. Some sentences and phrases and words may sound like "clanging symbols." This is a reminder that what looks good on paper for the eye may not sound good when spoken for the ear.

2. **Some material is boring.** When we deliver the sermon, there may be sections that do not excite us and we say them in unexciting ways. Sometimes, what we have prepared can have low interest value. Again, it might look good when we write it down, but when we speak it, we find it creating a yawn in ourselves. If the material is not easily pictured, if it does not excite us, if we cannot say it in an exciting way, chances are it is boring material. Re-work it, re-picture and re-image it, or just get rid of it.

3. **Some material is hard to remember.** No matter how hard we try, some parts of the sermon are just too hard to remember. We must honestly ask ourselves why that is so. Often it is because the material is not clear, not pictured in an interesting way. If we find a section hard to remember, seriously seek to re-work it. Find a better or clearer way to say it. Come up with new images, or pictures, or illustrations that capture the idea. If we go through the sermon three times and forget the same parts each time, that is a pretty good indication that those parts need to be re-thought and re-worked. If it is hard for us to remember, how easy would it be for our hearers to remember?

4. **Some material may be out of place.** As I practice the sermon, I often discover that I need to re-arrange some of the material. It is good material, but it would fit better in another place. The sermon needs to flow smoothly and naturally and if it does not, maybe the material is out of "sync." For example, maybe the story of the text should come after the question about God rather than before it. Or maybe that illustration would be more powerful after that section of application.

Do not be afraid to re-arrange the material if it would contribute to a smoother flow for the sermon. Sometimes if we have trouble remembering a section of the sermon, it may be because that section is not in the right place. If we move it to create a more natural flow for the sermon, it will then be easier to remember.

5. **Some new ideas and images may appear.** Quite often as we practice the sermon, new ideas and images come to the surface. I think this happens because we do think better on our feet. Some of these new ideas and images may be better than the ones we have. We may replace some of our images with the new ones. But this is not always the case. What we have already prepared may still be the best way to say it. But do not be surprised if new thoughts come. Pay attention to them and determine if they are useful.

As a side thought, often students ask about the new ideas that come to them sometimes as they are actually preaching the sermon. Should they bring these ideas into the sermon? Are they the promptings of the Spirit? No one can easily determine that. However, I try to remind them that there are a lot of "spirits" around today. The author of I John told the people to "test the spirits" to see which were from God and which were not (I John 4:1 ff). I feel that we should trust all the preparation that we have done. I feel the Holy Spirit works through all of that – from the study of the scripture, the getting of an idea, the construction of the sermon, even in the practice of it. For myself, I have always trusted the word I felt God had given to me through the hard work. Sometimes, when we direct our thinking away from what we have prepared, we can say what may not be well-thought through. Sometimes, this might get us into trouble. Trust the word we have gotten from God through all the serious study we have done.

Instant Replays

After the practice runs, between them and the time of preaching, I go through what I call "instant replays." I seek to let the sermon run through my mind at various times. It is like pushing the button on the movie projector and letting the images of the movie just pass by. These replays may only take a few moments. I try to recall the images for the sermon. If I do that, I feel confident I can describe the pictures the images suggest.

We will each develop our own unique ways and places for doing that. One of mine is the shower. As I take my shower, I often repeat the sermon out loud. (There is not an unconverted bar of soap or shampoo bottle in my shower.) I also like to lie alone in bed, listening to some soft background music, and let the sermon images flow through my mind. Wherever you feel comfortable, however it is best for you – allow the sermon to flash through your mind. Absorb it. Let it become a word you just have to preach. It must come out of you; you can keep it a secret no longer.

I must admit that I was not good company on Saturday nights. My basic rule was to not go out on Saturday nights. One reason for that was to make sure that I got the proper rest needed for Sunday. Preaching is hard work. It takes a toll on us physically, mentally, emotionally. We need to be physically ready to preach on Sunday. If we are tired, it will not enable us to preach our best.

The other reason I wanted to stay in on Saturday nights was because I was absorbing the sermon for the last time. It had become a part of me and had "taken me over." It was on my mind. That night, I just wanted to relax and rest, enjoy myself if I could. I would do an instant replay of the sermon the last thing before I went to bed and the first thing when I woke up on Sunday. My hope was that I was now deeply and intimately connected with the sermon. When I delivered it, I would be delivering myself. The sermon would seem to be a natural part of me. If that happened, passion would be behind the moment of delivery.

Here is a discovery. The fewer the interruptions from Saturday night to the moment of preaching, the better focused I was. Some interruptions can not be avoided. Try to minimize them. Get in touch with the sermon. Get it inside of you. Then when you preach, push the button on that movie projector and let the show begin.

A RECAP

I have tried to give some helps in this chapter for getting the sermon "inside" of us, to absorb it. There are two keys to this. Writing out the sermon is the first key. Write the "picture" column of the image outline. Having prepared that section really should make it easier and quicker to write.

Key two is practicing the sermon. We must discipline ourselves to do the work necessary to improve our delivery skills. Not only do we want to have something worthwhile to say, we want to say it in a worthwhile manner. Practicing the sermon will help us, not only to absorb the sermon, but to improve the way we say it.

In my experience, these keys have proved invaluable. Practicing the sermon has been a positive activity. I can say this. The more we do it, the better preachers we will become. And I also say this: it will get easier the more we do it.

---

1. Fred Craddock, *Preaching* (Nashville: Abingdon, 1985), 191-192.

2. Eugene Lowry, *Doing Time in the Pulpit* (Nashville: Abingdon, 1985), 102.

3. Clyde E. Fant, *Preaching for Today* (San Francisco: Harper and Row Publishers, 1987), 165 ff.

4. *Ibid.*, 166.

5. *Ibid.*, 167.

6. *Ibid.*, 170.

7. *Ibid.*, 171.

Chapter Six

Stepping Out: The Moment Of Truth

Do you remember the first time you dove off the high board? I remember it well. I had become a pretty good user of the low board. I had even done flips off it. But that high dive loomed there, silhouetted against that blue sky, beckoning me to dare come and jump off it. One day, through the encouragement of my friends – which usually came in phrases like, "Are you too chicken to jump off the high board?" – I nervously climbed up the steps to take that challenge. I slowly walked to the end – and made a mistake! I looked down at the water. It seemed 100 miles away! My knees began to buckle, my courage began to disappear. I was ready to turn and climb back down the ladder, but the way was blocked by my encouraging friends. I had stepped out on the diving board and there was no turning back. I had arrived at the moment of truth.

Now I had done a lot of diving from the low board. I knew how I was supposed to hit the water. I had hurled myself into space before – just not as much space. Leaning on my past experience, I felt that a feet-first dive would be wise and probably the safest one I could do. I took a deep breath, jumped up and down, and out I went. Down I flew, too fast it seemed, hitting the water feet first. Surprise! I made it! I didn't die! It wasn't a pretty dive, but it was an adequate one. I had done it! After that, I gained more confidence in my ability to dive from the high board. I made a lot of dives – some good, some bad – but I got to the place where I was able to dive well enough so no one would laugh at me.

Preaching without notes for the first time is similar to that experience. You have preached before and have gotten by fairly well. But there has always been that feeling that you could do it without notes, and if you did, you would be a more effective preacher. Finally, with some encouragement from others (like me), you want to try to see if you can do it. You have done the preparation, and now you have walked to the pulpit. The people are listening for your word. You stand there with not a note anywhere. Your knees begin to buckle, your courage begins to wane, your stomach is doing acrobatic tricks. But you can not go back. It is too late for that. It is time to step out and "dive" in. You have reached the moment of truth. How exciting – and how frightening it is!

Usually there are two feelings that students report that they have at that moment. One is the feeling of inadequacy. "I can't do it." That is not unusual. They have felt that way for a long time; that is why they had never tried it before. Such feelings are hard to kill. They are always lurking in the background, ready to pounce upon us. Do not be surprised when they appear.

The other feeling is that, "I will forget." As I said earlier, they might. I wish there was a guarantee I could give to assure them that they would not forget. There is none. However, from the experience of students across the years, forgetting does not happen all that much.

It is an anxiety-producing moment when we stand to preach without notes for the first time. One word I say about that is this: it is a time for trust.

A MATTER OF TRUST
In facing that first moment of preaching, there are some matters we need to trust.

Trust Our Preparation
We did not arrive at this moment easily. We took a long road to get there. When I dove off that high diving board, I had actually been preparing for it. All the many dives I had done off the low board were giving me some good experiences in making dives. I had talked to others about their experiences of high diving and learned from them. I had watched others do it and made mental notes from that. I had thought about it a lot. So when that moment came and I stood on the edge of the board and started to jump, a lot of thought and preparation had gone into it. To be truthful, that is

why I was there. With all the preparation for it, I was conf
that I could do it.

Following the preparation process I have outlined should have prepared us for this moment. We have thought a great deal about what we are going to say and how we are going to say it. We have outlined it, written it down, imaged it. We have practiced it out loud a number of times. We have thought about it a lot. All of that work has been making an impression on us, "carving" the sermon into our soul. In a way, when we get up to preach, we are going to introduce an "old friend" to the people. We are intimate friends with this sermon. We know it well. Preaching is that exciting moment when we get to tell others about this friend.

Trust the preparation! It has prepared us well for the moment. Have confidence that all we did was not in vain. We *do* know the sermon. We do have something to say.

Have you ever had this dream? We are standing before the congregation. It is time to preach. But we are standing before them not wearing one stitch of clothing. I have had that dream. I think I know what it means. It is about that ultimate fear we have as preachers that when we stand up before the people to preach, we will have nothing to say. The reason we have nothing to say is because we did not prepare.

That will not happen if we truly want to preach without notes. The price for such preaching is preparation. If we have prepared, we will have something to say. Trust all the work we have done before that moment. I feel it will not let us down.

Trust Our Abilities

If I did not have some athletic abilities, I would have never gotten up on that diving board. However, I had learned to swim and had discovered I could dive fairly well off the low board. I was not a total klutz. Since I had some abilities, I began to believe I also had the ability to jump off the high dive. If I did not trust my abilities, I never would have done it.

It is always good to remember this. God is the One who called us to preach. And God does not make any mistakes. Others have hopefully affirmed God's call to us, but God is the Caller. God knows that we have the needed abilities to serve the kingdom. God has given us gifts for ministry. We are needed – and we are able to do the work. If not, God's call to ministry would not have come.

We need to trust that call. At times, we need to push ourselves just to see what our gifts are. We may have the gift to preach without notes, but if we never try it, we may not know that. God has seen special talents in us for the work and has great confidence in our abilities. Maybe we should trust our own abilities.

Most of you are not going into this preaching moment "cold." You have been doing a lot of preaching and have found some success and affirmation in it. Now all you want to do is to build on that, to take it another step forward. You have been faithful in preaching with notes, now you can see if you might meet the challenge of preaching without notes.

I have found that a lot of us preachers have a low sense of self-esteem. We often doubt our abilities, doubt that we have any special gifts that could make a difference to God's work. May we never forget who called us! I feel that the God who called us is the God who will also empower and enable us to do the work. Maybe even to preach without notes!

Trust God

I can tell you that as I stood on that high dive ready to jump, I did a lot of praying. "Lord, help me not to kill myself. Help me not to make a fool of myself." When I stand in the pulpit each Sunday, I do a lot of praying then. "Lord, please be with me. Give me the strength. Help me not to make a fool of myself."

God has promised to be with us and I am sure that promise stretches to the pulpit. Preaching is a divine-human work. We bring all that we know how to do to the moment of preaching, and God meets us there in the power of the Spirit. God will honor all the work that we have done to preach the word. We must trust God to be with us and give us the power to do it. We are not alone in the pulpit.

I was serving a church as an interim and they had a sound system that was "fussy." I had to wear one of those clip-on mikes, but I could never tell if it was on or off. Because of loose wires and such, it often cut off as I was preaching. One Sunday I had started to preach and was going after it. All of a sudden, I felt something brush against my leg. I looked down and there was – Ralph! I wish I could have taken a picture of his face as he was looking up at me. Shocked, I cried out, "My soul, there's a man up here!" I discovered that my mike had gone dead and Ralph had sneaked down from the choir, gotten on his hands and knees to try to slip by me and wriggle some of the wires in the pulpit, hoping to get the mike to work. Most everyone in the congregation had seen Ralph slipping down. What a surprise to me to discover that I was not alone in the pulpit!

Truthfully, we never are. The Spirit of Christ is with us, helping us, encouraging us, strengthening us. We need to depend on that. In my judgment, it is a "given" of the faith. If we are serious in seeking to proclaim the Word of God, God will be faithful to us. We need to trust that Presence with us. Let God calm our fears and give us a sense of confidence. Maybe God can get those "butterflies" in our stomachs to "fly in formation," as the old saying goes. Trust God to be there with us.

SOME HOPEFULLY HELPFUL HINTS

In a continuing effort to help relieve the anxiety of the preaching moment, I offer these hopefully helpful hints. (Notice the clever use of alliteration. In sermons, try to avoid such overdone alliteration.)

1. **Minimize interruptions before preaching.**

Reminding us of what I emphasized in the last chapter, we need to really focus in on our sermon on Sunday morning (or whenever we preach). Usually before breakfast, I ran through the images of the sermon in my mind. If I could remember the images, then I felt confident that I could describe the pictures they suggested. When I got to the church, the hour before the worship service I tried to spend in my study. I wanted it to be a quiet time, a time of meditation, of brooding over the sermon, a time of preparing myself personally for the preaching moment. As far as possible, I would schedule no appointments during that time. I was trying to minimize the interruptions.

123

Interruptions will occur. We need to be available to respond to the legitimate needs of others. But we do need to find a few quiet moments for ourselves where we can run through the sermon one last time. Clyde Fant used to tell us that when he got into the study for those moments, the only way people could interrupt him was for them to be either dead or dying, and they had to be able to give evidence of both. We must find that quiet moment to prepare ourselves for the awesome responsibility before us.

Usually before the service, a lot of people will want to come and have a "quick word" with us. I tried to make sure that such words were important. When they wanted to talk about the potluck supper, or the proposed constitutional amendment, or the program of the men's meeting, I would tell them that I would call them on Monday. I could not spend my energy talking about such matters just before the time of preaching the word.

Find the best method for you, but try to minimize the interruptions. Focus in on the message.

2. Know the beginning of the sermon.

Often the hardest part is starting out. If we can get going, then usually all the preparation we have done will take over. Throwing those first words over the chasm that seems to separate the people from us — that is the tough part. So I encourage you to know that introduction well. If you have to memorize the first few lines, do that. Be confident that you can start out.

I find it best to use easily remembered material here. An illustration or a personal experience are often excellent openers. Not only are they easier to picture and thus remember, but they also have high interest value. Connecting with the hearers "right off the bat" is accomplished.

Know the beginning. I also add, make sure you know the "signposts." If you do forget, if you can remember what part or section of the sermon you are in, you might be able to remember what comes next.

3. Start with simply-organized sermons.

In our first efforts at preaching without notes, it may be best to start with sermons that are easily organized. The more simply organized, the easier it will be to recall. There are several possibilities.

A. Biographical Sermon

This is a sermon that deals with the life, or some events in the life, of a biblical character. We tell the story of the character and then apply that story to our people. This can be done in a couple of ways.

1. **Tell the story, then draw a truth from it.**

We select a character and then tell the story about him/her. After we tell the story, then we seek to draw analogies that apply to our lives today. In dealing with the event when David killed Goliath, we tell that story, then we talk about how we can kill our Goliaths. We explain, then we apply.

I.   Explanation: David killed Goliath when he depended on God.

II. Application: We can kill our Goliaths when we depend on God.

Such a sermon has two main sections. That should make it easier to remember.

2. **Divide the story, explaining and applying as we go.**

In this type, we tell the story of David and Goliath, but we divide it into sections, or points, or scenes. We tell part of the story, apply it, then tell another part.

I.   God gives us courage for the fight.

Exp: God gave David courage.

App: God will give us courage.

II. God gives us gifts for the fight.

Exp: David used his sling, his skill.

App: God will help us use our strengths.

III. God gives us strength for the fight.

Exp: God gave David strength to win.

App: God will give us strength to win.

B. Narrative Sermon

Similar to the biographical sermon is the narrative approach. This tells some story from the text and weaves the sermon around it. It could focus around a character, like David; or an event, like the Exodus; or an idea, like forgiveness. The sermon tells the story and seeks to apply its meaning to now. One way to do it is to divide the story into three sections:

    I. God's story – the story in the Bible

    II. Our story – how that story matters to us

    III. Their story – how the story can matter to them

      Maybe we are preaching on the parable of the prodigal son, then we can arrange the sermon:

    I. God's story: the young boy took his money, left home, ruined his life, came to his senses in a pigsty, went home and found a father's love.

    II. Our story: we know that story. We have rebelled and run from God. Made a mess of our lives. But when we came back to God, we found love and forgiveness.

    III. Their story: Have you run from God? Rebelled against God? You have made a mess of your life and want to come back? There is a God waiting for you with arms of love and forgiveness. You can go back home.

    The idea is to have a simple road map that is easy to follow. Narrative sermons can give that.

C. Problem/Solution Sermon

    This is one of the easiest ways to organize a sermon. We talk about a problem and then find the biblical solution for it. It makes for an easy outline.

    I. Problem: David faced the giant.

    II. Solution: God helped David defeat the giant.

    In doing such a sermon, make sure you spend as much time dealing with the solution as you do the problem. Too many sermons are ninety percent problem, ten percent good news. It should be at least 50-50. When push comes to shove, I prefer more solution than problem.

D. Use Familiar Texts

We all have our favorite texts, texts that we know inside and out. It might be good to use these texts for our first stabs at preaching without notes. Such texts we will not forget. They have meant a great deal to us, and our sermons can share why.

The key is not to make it hard on ourselves by constructing complex, difficult sermons that will be hard to remember. In the beginning, strive for simplicity in sermon structure.

4. Start on a less threatening occasion.

By this I mean that the time for the first sermon without notes probably should not be Easter Sunday. There may be other times when there will not be as much pressure as that Sunday presents.

A Sunday night service is a possibility, if your church has one. Usually there are not as many people there. One pastor said that if they canceled Sunday night services at his church it would be six months before most of the people found out about it. Most pastors can understand that statement. Those who come are the "faithful few" who will love us, no matter how well – or how badly – we preach. It might be a good time to try a sermon without notes. There is less pressure and the people will be supportive.

If you have a Wednesday night time of preaching, you could try it then. Or a Sunday during the summer months when everyone seems to be more relaxed and easier to get along with.

Start out on a Sunday that you will feel comfortable, that will not add any undue pressure on you.

5. Preach a shorter sermon.

It might be heresy to suggest this, but for the first few times, we might shorten the sermon. If we are used to preaching 25-30 minutes, try 15-20. The value in that is that there will not be as much material to remember. We can find a manageable amount and limit the sermon to that.

After some good experiences with shorter sermons, then we can expand them if we need to. Although, what we might discover is that our people really do enjoy our shorter sermons. I have seldom had someone complain because my sermons were too short. Sometimes, less is more.

6. **Keep the three functional uses of language central.**

The three functions of our language in a sermon are to explain ideas, apply the ideas, and illustrate the ideas. As we begin to preach without notes, we can keep the development of our sermon/ sermon points that simple. After each signpost, we simply explain the text, apply the truth of it to now, illustrate it, and then get on to the next section. All we have to keep in mind are those functions – explanation, application, and illustration. We do not need to "pad" our sermons with a lot of "filler" statements. State the truth clearly and then move on. Do not be too wordy.

7. **Eliminate quotes and poetry.**

I hear a lot of sermons that are crammed full of quotes and poems. In preaching without notes, we will probably have to eliminate these. It is putting extra pressure on us to try to memorize a quote or several lines of poetry. For that is what we would have to do if they are to be presented correctly. Do we want to spend time memorizing such material?

There are really only two reasons to use a quote. One is if the quote says the truth in such a way that it can not be restated in a better way. The second is if the person quoted has such instant credibility that to use a quote from that person would add authority to the sermon.

Very seldom is there a quote so perfect that it cannot be paraphrased or restated in another way. Once in a while, the name of the person will enhance the sermon, but not all that much. In my judgment, too many quotes bog down a sermon and slow down its smooth flow. I do not think it is best to use them. However, if it is so powerful that it must be used, my suggestion is to write it down on a 5" by 7" card and take it into the pulpit and then to read it. Do not try to hide the fact that we are reading it. Practice reading it well, with feeling and emphasis. This way we will not put on ourselves the pressure of having to memorize it, a pressure we do not need. If we read it effectively, it can still carry a powerful impact.

As for poetry, if that must be used, do the same with it. Read it; do not try to memorize it. And please, practice reading it beforehand, seeking to present it with all the feeling and meaning and emphasis of the writer. In listening to sermons, I have discovered that we do not read poetry too well. Too many poems are delivered in a "sing-song" manner, not really capturing the essence of the poem. Poetry is the language of the emotions. If we use poems, read them like a poet would do – dramatically, and with feeling.

8. Concentrate on the moment, not the future.

Sometimes when I am preaching, I let my mind begin to wander – what's up ahead? Do I remember it? When I let myself think that, I usually get into trouble. I begin to panic. Just what is it that I planned to say?

I have discovered that I need to be totally focused on what I am saying at the moment, not worrying about what is to come. Since I have worked hard to prepare a sermon that flows naturally, I will usually have no trouble "flowing" into what is next. This is what all that practice was for. We have gotten the "feel" of it and when we preach it, it will come to us naturally. A will lead to B, and B will lead to C, etc. When we are speaking about A, it is best not to let our minds jump ahead to think about C. Concentrate on the point at hand and trust that when it is time for the next point to show up, it will.

9. We can prepare the people for it.

It is not too bad an idea to let some people in on the secret that we are going to try something new with our preaching. We might tell the deacons or elders, some church leaders, or even the whole church what we are going to try. We want to try to preach without notes. We do not know if we can, but we want to see. We can even ask them to pray for us. I think our people will be glad to encourage us and to pray for us. They might secretly be glad that we are going to try to preach without notes. I always have to keep reminding myself that the people in the church are not my enemies. They are my sisters and brothers in Christ and most of them are more than willing to come along side of me and help me do ministry. That probably is true for your people, too. We at least can give them the chance to support us. Besides, if we tell them we are going to try it and then forget something, they will understand and be sympathetic. They will pull for you.

10. **If we forget, admit it.**

Let's suppose that the worst scenario happens. We start preaching and then – boom! The mind goes blank! We can not remember anything! Yes, we will feel embarrassed about that. If it happens – and my guess is that it will not – my suggestion is to go ahead and admit it. Say something like, "As some of you know, I was trying something new this Sunday. I was trying to preach without notes, but I am afraid I have forgotten what I was going to say. I wanted to try it, but I guess I am not ready for it yet. I'm sorry. Come back next Sunday and maybe I will remember."

People will be forgiving and understanding. I would also venture that some will come and encourage us to keep on trying. Even though we could not do it this time, they will tell us that we might be able to do it the next time. Most of them would like to see us be able to do it.

To forget one Sunday will not be the worst thing that could happen to us. The calendar is very forgiving; it just tells us that another Sunday is coming. Get ready for that one.

11. **If we forget something, worry not.**

We made it through the sermon. We remembered enough of it. We did not fall on our faces. Then we go and look over the manuscript. We make some interesting discoveries. We forgot to say that idea, we left out that illustration, or we skipped the text there. Do not fret. Remember, we are the only ones who know we left that stuff out. They had not read our sermon. They did not miss anything or say after the sermon, "You left out that story about the dog." We are the only ones who know.

If it is important material, here is our saving grace. There are 51 more Sundays in the year. Surely we can work those ideas in on one of them.

12. **"Cheat" a little.**

I am reluctant even to make this suggestion, but I am trying to be practical. Some of you may really want to try preaching without notes, but you just can not seek to break away from having that "security blanket" of notes in the pulpit. You want to try – but! I will offer this compromise. Take into the pulpit an outline of the image words, but put it someplace where you can not see it. Try preaching without it. But if you truly get lost and can not remember the sermon for the life of you, then you can look at the outline. You will have that "crutch" with you if you honestly need it. But if you do not, it is out of sight.

13. Be realistic in expectations.

I have had students preach without notes and come back excited about it. It was going to revolutionize their preaching. They had a good experience.

I have had other students who did not have that grand an experience. They stumbled through it, or forgot some major parts, or mixed the sermon up. They were not so sure they should try to do it again.

Be realistic in your expectations for yourself. This is not a skill that can be easily acquired overnight. It takes time and experience to arrive at the place where you will be comfortable with it. If you have a good first experience, rejoice and be glad. But do not neglect to do the work needed to be able to do it the second time. If you have a hard experience with it, do not get too discouraged. It is like trying to learn how to ride a horse. If you get thrown off the first time, it does not mean you can not ride it. You need to get back in the saddle and try again. It would be a mistake to give up too quickly.

It could be that you might have to take this preaching journey in several steps. One step is to take the full image outline into the pulpit with you. Depend on that for a while. Get comfortable preaching from that outline.

After a period of time, take the next step. Take only the image words with you. Work on that for a few months. When you reach the stage when you can preach confidently from just the image words, it may be the time to move on and try it without notes.

You know yourself and your abilities better than I do. Choose your own pace, set your own timetable. Be realistic about your expectations. It may take several months to a year to begin to get comfortable with the system. If you "blow" one sermon, go after it in the next one. Do not give up too quickly. My conviction is that more preachers can do this than think they can. You might be one of them.

A RECAP

This chapter has sought to deal with that moment when we try to preach without notes for the first time. It is an anxiety-filled time. As we do it, we must trust the preparation we have done, trust the abilities God gave us to do it, and above all, trust the promise that God will be with us in the doing of it.

If we never "step out" and try it, we may never know what we can do. The moment of truth has now arrived. Step out!

Chapter Seven

The Final Word: Now What?

Well, how did it go? Oh, you haven't tried it yet? Do me a favor. Before reading this chapter, give it a try. See what happens and then come and join me again on this page.

GREAT!

Well, how did it go? It went well! Great! You made it through. You did not forget anything important. You told your stories well. And the people really seemed to be with you. It was an exciting experience.

Congratulations! You are now among those who know what it is to preach without notes. You have discovered that you have the ability to do it. It is no longer out of reach for you. That should make you feel good about yourself.

I hope it was fun. I hope you felt the freedom that such preaching can bring – freedom from notes, freedom to see the people, freedom to respond to them as they reacted to what you were saying. It is a great feeling! There come those moments when you feel at one – with God and with the people. May that experience enliven your preaching!

What now? Keep at it! Go for it the second time, then the third, and beyond. Since you now know you can do it, that challenges you with the responsibility to be a good steward of that gift. Make a commitment to preach without notes all the time. You know you can do it. So – go and do it!

RATS!

How did it go? Not so well? It was not a great experience for you. You forgot too much. There were too many long and awkward pauses as you tried to remember what you were supposed to say.

You stammered and stumbled through too many words. You were relieved when it was over. You think that maybe you just cannot do this. It was a terrifying moment for you.

Well, rats! I'm sorry. What now? One thing to do is to try and figure out why it did not go so well. Was the material too complicated to remember? Was the sermon too confusing, not flowing well? Was it just too frightening to you that your nerves were shot? Did you need to prepare better? Try to take an honest look at why it may not have gone so well.

After you have that experience that causes you to want to say, "Rats!" there are three possible roads to take.

1. **It is just not your style.** That could be very true. As I have repeatedly said, preaching without notes is not for everyone. Many are tremendously effective preachers who read their sermons word for word, or who preach from an extensive outline, or from a short one. There is nothing wrong with that. Each of us has to find out what gifts we have for preaching and fit our style to those gifts. The key idea to remember is that however we preach, we must work hard at being an effective communicator through that mode.

If you do not think you can preach without notes, do not feel discouraged about that. Feel good about the fact that you tried to see if you could. That's a courageous step to take. Through it all, you have discovered a lot about yourself and your preaching abilities and style. I wish you the best as you pursue your preaching ministry.

2. **Go from an outline.** Maybe you feel that you could go from an outline. You do not feel comfortable without any notes, but you feel that with just a few notes, you would be all right.

Go for that! After all of this preparation process, I would encourage you to go with just the "image words" outline. See if you can get by with just those words. If you see them, you can describe the pictures they suggest without any difficulty. If you can go with just that outline, you are almost preaching without notes. Your delivery will be much improved.

Try it and see. But if you need the full image outline, go with it. Experiment! See what feels most comfortable to you. The less you need to depend on notes, the better. Continue to go through the preparation process presented in this book. It will give you the outline needed for the sermon. I wish you the best as you develop your preaching ministry.

3. **Time to try again.** Even though you had a tough first experience, there is still something inside you that tells you not to give up. You can do it – you just need to try again. Maybe you need a more simply constructed sermon. Or better images. Or more time to practice and absorb it. But you still think you can do it.

Go for it! Try it again – and again. Give yourself a fair shot at it. Try it several times. After several times, if you still can not do it, maybe you need to fall back on another method. But if you still want to do it, and think you can, persevere! You might have to make some adaptations and changes on my process in order to help it better fit you. Well and good! Whatever it takes to see if you can do it, I wish you well in your continuing efforts to preach without notes.

A POSSIBLE ACROSTIC?

We have taken a long journey together and have covered a lot of ground. I hope it has been a pleasant trip for you. I have enjoyed trying to share what I know. I have sought ways to try to make it clear and easy to understand. I hope I have succeeded.

In other works, I have seen writers put their ideas into acrostics to help the ideas to be easily remembered. Try as I may, I could not come up with a "cute" one. If I had to put the ideas into one, it would be S.P.I.A. What do those letters signify?

Simplify – get a clear road map for the sermon. One thesis that leads to one objective. The clearer, the better. The more simply organized, the better.

Picturing – see the ideas coming to life in our minds. Picture the text happening again. Picture the idea coming to life among our people. Picture the illustrations that throw light on the idea. In a way, we picture the scenes, step into them, and describe to others what we see. We become witnesses. We just testify to what we see.

Imaging –   seek to condense the pictures into an image of a word or two. If we can remember the image, we will recall the picture and be able to describe it.

Absorb –   strive to get the sermon "out there" *into* us. Through writing and practicing out loud, we want to absorb the sermon, let it get into our "blood streams" and become a part of us. The sermon should not be out there on a piece of paper, but should be coming from inside us.

So there you have the letters – SPIA. I have thought and thought about what these letters could mean. I have only come up with one idea. Stand back – here it comes! SPIA – the Society for the Prevention of Insomnia in Audiences. Clever, right? OK, so it is sort of sickening. It is the best I can do. Maybe you can come up with a better thought. Let me know if you can.

With that foolishness aside, I just say to you that I have written this book because I wanted to share with you the joy and excitement I feel in preaching without notes. For me, it brings life to my preaching. I still stumble around at times. I use the wrong verb tense, or mispronounce a word, or split an infinitive badly. But most of the people do not seem to mind. I sense the freedom to preach – to stand before the people free to look at them and respond to them and to share with them the word God has allowed me to speak. My hope is that some of you can experience that sense of freedom in your preaching days ahead.

Someone told me the story of a boy who heard that the community band was looking for a trombone player. He went down and told the director that he would like to be the trombone player. The director was excited to hear that, since they were marching in a parade the next day. He gave the boy a uniform and told him to show up the next day. He did and they began to march in the parade. When they started to play the music, awful sounds were heard from the trombone section. The boy could not play the trombone! The director asked him, "Why didn't you tell me you couldn't play the trombone?" The boy answered, "Well, I didn't know. I had never tried it before."

I like that boy's spirit. He may have had the potential to be the world's greatest trombone player, but if he never tried it, he would have never known. Some of us may have the potential to be the world's greatest trombone player, or writer, or baseball player, but we have never tried it.

This is what this book has been about. Trying – seeing if we can preach without notes. Hopefully, we now know what our potential is. Whatever it is, however we preach, may God's blessing be upon us. And always – to God be the glory!

Three Sermons

To Illustrate The Imaging Process

Sermon 1: A Word For Willie

This was the sermon I used in the book as an illustration of the imaging process. It contains elements of both inductive and deductive sermon development. The sermon was preached to a local church congregation.

COVER PAGE

Title: A Word for Willie
Text: John 8:2-11
CIT: Jesus did for the woman what no one else could.
Thesis: Jesus will do for us what no one else will.
GO: Evangelistic
SO: That they will trust Jesus to meet their every need.
Signposts:
    I.   Jesus Will Love Us When No One Else Will.
   II.   Jesus Will Forgive Us When No One else Will.
  III.   Jesus Will Believe In Us When No One Else Will.

IMAGE OUTLINE

IDEA	PICTURE	IMAGE
Introduction		
1. What is so special about Jesus?	Willie asked me, "What is so special about Jesus?"	Willie's question
2. Can we answer that question?	Answer?	Answer?
3. What would be an answer for us?	Giving an answer	Word for Willie
4. Text: Religious leaders asked about the woman caught in adultery	Text story	Text
5. How does the text answer the question?	Jesus' answer	Jesus' answer
I. Love		
1. Jesus stood up for the woman when no one else would	Text	Text
2. Hear it, but don't believe it	Love heard in church	Disbelief
3. Feel we don't deserve it	Woman felt unworthy	Woman
4. Try to earn it	Man, active in church	Churchworker
5. Can't be earned or deserved	Love ours already	Are loved
6. Daughter	Daughter	Daughter
7. Love never stops	Love keeps coming for us all	Unstoppable

141

II. Forgiveness

1. Jesus forgave the woman	Text	Text
2. We don't believe forgiveness is real	People can't forgive themselves	Unbelievable
3. God forgives through Christ	Cross event	Cross
4. Forgiveness for all sins	Future is most important	Clean slate
5. Bishop's sin	Bishop	Bishop
6. Forgiveness is the gospel	Forgiven!	Forgiven!

III. Belief

1. Jesus believed in her future	Text	Text
2. Feel we can't improve	Can't	Can't
3. Jesus encourages us	Can	Can
4. Jesus will help us	Let Jesus help us	Help
5. Sculptor	Sculptor	Sculptor
6. Jesus will bless what we do	Master Sculptor	Master Sculptor

Conclusion

1. Recess ended, Willie left	Willie	Willie
2. Summary of what I had said	Summary	Summary
3. Willie's fate	Fate	Fate
4. Do we believe it?	Decision	Decision

142

IMAGE	Sermon content
Willie's question	Before I went to seminary, I taught the sixth grade and in that class of 11-year olds, there was a red-headed, freckle-faced 15-year-old boy named Willie. Willie was the kind of student that was always in trouble, always winding up in the principal's office. He was the kind of boy that, if he was absent, the day went by smoothly. But if he was there, it was a long hard day. Not many had a good word for Willie. I wanted to understand him better, so I did some research about his life. I discovered that Willie was the product of a broken home, several times over. Throughout his life, Willie had been an abused and neglected child. Willie felt that no one cared too much for him.

One day at recess, Willie came over to me. He knew that I would soon be headed off to seminary to study to become a preacher. He said, "I want to ask you something. All my friends say that what I need to do to solve my problems is to go to church and to believe in Jesus. I don't see why. I know these friends and believing in Jesus doesn't seem to do too much for them. Maybe you can tell me. What's so special about Jesus?"

Answer?

Well, what would you tell him? What would be your word for Willie? Maybe you wonder the same thing. You have heard about Jesus a lot and you hear others talking about how you need to "believe in Jesus." But you do not know why. Why should you? Just what is it that is so special about Jesus?

Word for Willie

I want to tell you what I told Willie that day in the schoolyard. I want to give you my word for Willie and for any of you who are asking that question. What is so special about Jesus?

143

Text	In the story from the scripture, we can find the answer. The New Testament writers tried to tell us why Jesus was so special through the stories they told. So we have this story. Here is the scene. Jesus was teaching the people and the religious leaders brought a woman to Him who had been caught in the act of adultery. There was no doubt about that. Now the Law of Moses dictated that those caught in adultery, both the man and the woman, should be stoned to death. These religious leaders were ready to carry out that sentence. But they made a mistake! They asked Jesus what He would do.
Jesus' answer	What did Jesus do? As we see what Jesus did, we can begin to get an answer to our question. What is so special about Jesus?
Love	I. Jesus is Special Because He Will Love Us When No One Else Will.
Text	A woman was caught in the act of adultery. No doubt about that. The Law of Moses said that when that happened, both the man (who seems to be missing here) and the woman were to be stoned to death. These religious leaders were ready to carry out that sentence. They had the stones in their hands. But they made a mistake! They brought her to Jesus and asked Him, "What should we do with her?" Now notice. Nobody seemed to reach out to this woman. No one seemed to try to understand why she did what she did. Not one of the religious leaders seemed to have any compassion for her. In fact, the only reason they brought her to Jesus was so they might trick Him into making some mistake, going against the Law, or against them. If He did that, then they could "get" Him. This

144

woman was nothing but a pawn in their hands, a "thing" to be used at their desire. They did not care about her.

To their question, Jesus said nothing, just bent down and wrote something on the ground. They grew impatient. "Come on, man, what do you want us to do with her?" Finally, Jesus rose, looked at them and said, "Let the one who has no sin throw the first stone." And no one could! Instead, the stones dropped to the ground as, one by one, they shuffled off.

Do you see what Jesus is doing here? He is standing up for this woman. He is defending her, watching out for her, caring for her. The religious leaders did not care, but Jesus did! This woman mattered to Him. It was for people like her that He had come in the first place. She mattered! No one else cared about her, but Jesus did!

Disbelief

Now we have heard all about that. We know that Jesus loves us. We talk about it all the time in church. We sing about it. We know that! But do we truly believe it? I am not too sure we do. As I have moved among people, I am coming to believe that we find God's love hard to accept. It seems too good to be true. Do you believe it? Do you really believe that God loves you?

Woman

I talked to a woman who had not lived too fine a life. She said to me that she was sure God could not love her. "After some of the things that I've done, there is no way that God could love me. I don't deserve the love of God." And she was right! None of us do. But she misunderstood that love. God's love for us does not depend on our deserving it. It depends on the grace of God that wants to give it – no matter what.

145

Churchworker   Or here was the man who was an active churchworker. Every time the doors of the church were open, he was there. Sunday morning, Sunday night, Wednesday night prayer service. If there was a committee that needed him, he was ready and willing to serve. If anything needed to be done, he stood up to do it. Someone asked him once, "Why do you do so much for the church? You are always there, giving so much of your time. Why?" And he answered, "Because I want to keep on the right side of God."

Do you hear what he was saying? He thought that if he kept doing good works for God, then somehow he would keep God loving him. But he was wrong! He was wrong because no matter how many good works he did, he could never earn the love of God. The reason? He already had it!

Are loved   This is the amazing truth of the gospel. We do not deserve the love of God – but no matter! It still comes to us. We can not earn the love of God – but no matter! It is ours for the believing, for the trusting. No matter who we are and what we have done, here is the good news – for Willie, for you, for me. We are loved! Do you hear that? Do you believe that?

Daughter   A minister told of the time his daughter came to him in his office with a strange paper. On two sheets of paper were written 100 times the words, "I will not talk in school." As she showed him the paper, he looked at her face and noticed how pale she was. She had been hiding from him all day. He looked at her and said, "Sarah, how long have you carried this paper around with you?" She said, "For two days, and I have to get your signature on it." He said, "Why didn't you bring it to me sooner?" She said, "I was afraid of you." "What could you have been afraid of?" "I can't really tell you," she said. He persisted. "Were you afraid that I would beat you?" "Of course not." "Afraid that I would scold you?" "No." "Afraid that I would preach to you?" He then said, "Sarah, let me tell you something. If you were so bad that your picture was on the front page of all the newspapers as the epitome of everything we should not be, I would not love you any less. Conversely, if your picture was on the front page of every newspaper as a model of what everyone should be, I would not love you any more. Do you understand that?" She looked at him and said, "You see, that's what I was afraid of. You always tell me things that don't make any sense."[1]

Unstoppable

And it does not make any sense, does it? Here comes the love of God in Jesus, and no matter what we do in response to it – ignore it, reject it, laugh at it, put it on a cross and crucify it – there is one thing we can never do to it. We can never stop it! Here it comes – to Willie, to you, to me. No matter what we have been or done, it comes and puts its arms around us and says, "We are loved!" No one else will love us like that, but Jesus will. Do you believe it? Want it? Trust it?

Forgiveness

II. Jesus is Special Because He Will Forgive Us When No One Else Will.

Text

Jesus turns to the woman. "Where are the ones who accuse you?" "They are all gone," she replied. "Neither do I condemn thee." Did you hear that? Here is a woman guilty of the terrible sin of adultery, and here is Jesus saying to her, "Forgiven!" They would not forgive her. No one would – except for Jesus. He did!

147

Unbelievable Jesus forgives us of our sins. We know that, too. We talk about it, sing about it, in our prayers we always ask for "the forgiveness of our sins." We know all about it – but do we believe it is true? Again, I am not so sure. This is another idea that seems to be too good to be true. Let me ask you: do you feel God will forgive you of your sin?

I have talked to many through the years who tell the same old story. They committed some terrible sins in the past and they are still plagued by guilt because of them. That guilt robs them of sleep at night. "Have you asked God to forgive you?" I ask. "Oh, yes," they say. "But we just feel God can't forgive us for what we've done."

There you have it. Unbelief! Feeling that forgiveness may be for others, but not for them. Do you ever feel like that? Your sin is so terrible that not even God can forgive it?

Cross But if there is one thing I am sure God was serious about, it was the forgiveness of sin. So serious was God that Jesus was sent to die on the cross for them. The death of Christ was not too high a price for God to pay to bring us forgiveness. Forgiveness is real! Whenever we do not think it is, we make a mockery of that cross. God was serious. Forgiveness is available for us if we want it.

Clean slate Why is it that some of us are still punishing ourselves for sins that God has long since forgiven? We do not have to punish ourselves. Don't we see? God is more concerned about what we will become than in what we have done. No matter what we have done, no matter how terrible it might have been, in Christ God says, "O.K. Let's forget about that and move on. Let's leave the mistakes behind and live for Me now." And

148

God says that to you, to me, to Willie and all the Willies of the world. No one else may care to forgive, but Jesus will!

Bishop

One of my Catholic friends told me a story that was making the rounds among them. A certain nun had a vision of Christ; Christ appeared to her. The Bishop had to go and "check out" the validity of that vision. "So Christ appeared to you?" he asked. "Yes," she answered. "And not only that, Christ told me that He was going to come and visit me again." The Bishop had an idea. He told her, "Before I became a Bishop, I committed a terrible sin. The only one who would know what it was besides me would be Christ. If He comes to visit you again, ask Him what was the Bishop's terrible sin." "I'll do that," she said. The Bishop left, thinking he had taken care of that matter.

However, a few months later, the nun called and wanted to see the Bishop. Christ had appeared to her again. Nervously, the Bishop drove down to see her. "So Christ appeared to you again?" "Yes." "Well, did you remember to ask Him that question I wanted you to ask?" "Oh, yes. You wanted me to ask Him what your terrible sin was." "Did you?" "Yes, I did." Now, quite nervously, the Bishop asked, "What did Jesus say?" And the nun replied, "Jesus said that He had forgotten!"

Forgiven!

Did you hear that? That is the gospel! For you, for me, for Willie. God is more concerned about what we will become than in punishing us for our past sins. Listen! Forgiveness is real! No one else may forgive us, but we can bet our lives that Jesus will!

149

Belief	**III. Jesus is Special Because He Believes In Us When No One Else Will.**
Text	Did you notice what Jesus said to this woman? After He had forgiven her, He said, "Go, and sin no more!" Now do you think she did? Of course. Everybody sins. But do you think she ever went back to the way of life she had been living? How could she, we wonder? Here she was, facing death and is given life. Guilty, but is given forgiveness. In despair, but she is given hope. How could she stay the same? Some scholars feel this woman was Mary Magdalene, who became one of the devoted followers of Jesus. Whatever happened to this woman? We can't say, but we do know one thing. Jesus believed in her and in her future. He believed that she could live a life that was better than the one she had lived. She could become more than she had ever been. Why? Because she had met Jesus. Jesus would make a difference in her life and help her become more than she had ever dreamed. No one else believed in her, but Jesus did!
Can't	Do we think we can become more than we are, do more than we have done? Too often, we do not think so. Too often the words that direct our lives are the words, "I can't." "I can't overcome that bad habit." "I can't teach that Sunday School class." "I can't keep my marriage together." "I can't be a missionary." On it goes. We look at the future and it seems to us to be impossible. Our best years have already been. We can not do more than we have done, or be more than we have been.
Can	Are we really sure? For all the time we are saying that we can't, Jesus is behind us saying, "Yes, you can!" And the reason Jesus says that

is because He will help us do it. We face the future with the promise of His help. He will be with us. So we can't overcome that bad habit? Have we honestly sought to let Christ help us overcome it? Or we can't keep our marriage together? Have both of you sincerely sought God's help in that? Or you can't be a missionary? Are you seeking God's help there?

Jesus believes in us and in our future. We can do more than we ever dreamed. Willie could become more than he ever thought if he would trust Christ to help him. So can we. There is no telling what amazing things we can accomplish when we put our total trust in Christ. Are we willing to take a risk and see what Christ will accomplish with us, through us?

Sculptor

I heard of an old man who had been a master sculptor in his day. He still liked to work with the clay, but his eyes were not as good and his hands shook. He would work for a while with the clay, and then he would stand back and look at what he had done. "That's ugly," he would say. "I'm never going to do that again." But that night while he was sleeping, his son – now the master sculptor – would go into the room and look at what his father had done. Then with his skilled hands, he would make a move there, an adjustment here. So in the morning, when his father walked into the room, he would look at the statue and say, "You know, that's not as bad as I thought." And back he would go to work some more with the clay.

Master Sculptor

Sometimes as we look at what we have been able to do for God, we say, "That's ugly. It makes no difference. We are never going to do that again." But all the while, Jesus, the Master Sculptor, takes what we have done, and with His

151

skilled hands, makes a move here, an adjustment there, and makes out of what we have done something magnificent. If we will trust God with our lives and our service day by day, one day we will be able to look back on what we have become, and what we have done for Jesus, and we will be amazed. Jesus will give us a magnificent future if we put our trust in Him.

Conclusion

Willie

Well, the bell rang and recess was over. It was time to go. Willie thanked me and said he would think about what I had said.

Summary

That was what I told him that day – and what I have been trying to tell others ever since. Willie, Jesus is special because He will love you when no one else will. You matter to Him. You are special! And Jesus will forgive you when no one else will. Willie, whatever you've done can be left behind. Jesus is more interested in today than yesterday. And if you trust this Jesus, He will help you to become more than you have ever dreamed. The possibilities are unlimited for your future if you let Jesus help you live it. Life can become an exciting adventure.

Fate

I asked Willie several times after that, "Have you thought about what we talked about?" He always said, "I'm still thinking about it." Well, school ended and I went a thousand miles away to seminary and lost touch with Willie. A few years ago, I found out what happened to him. Willie had dropped out of school, joined the armed forces, went to a place called Vietnam. And there – Willie died!

Decision

When I heard that, I hoped in my soul that what I told Willie that day in that schoolyard, somehow he believed. And I hope you do. The word for Willie is a word for every one of us. There is no one who will love us, forgive us, believe in us like Jesus. Do you believe that? Will you trust Him to do that for you?

---

1. David H. C. Read, sermon, *National Radio Pulpit*, July-August-September, 1972, 15-16.

Sermon 2: A Dinosaur In The Manger

This is a sermon in which I tried to use the inductive approach. It was a "problem/solution" type. It was initially delivered at a chapel service at the North American Baptist Seminary. Hence the application to seminary students. I also attempted to provide a new metaphor for the understanding of Christmas.

COVER PAGE

Title: A Dinosaur in the Manger

Text: Matthew 2:3-20

CIT: God delivered Jesus from his enemies.

Thesis: God will deliver us from our modern-day enemies.

GO: Supportive

SO: That they will trust God to deliver them from their enemies.

Signposts:

    I.   Problem: Herod – The Terror We Face

   II.   Solution: Jesus – The Victor Over All

IMAGE OUTLINE

IDEA	PICTURE	IMAGE
Introduction		
1. A dinosaur in the manger	Dinosaur	Dinosaur
2. There is a dinosaur in the Christmas story: Herod	Herod	Herod

I. Problem: Herod – The Terror We Face

IDEA	PICTURE	IMAGE
1. Text: Herod's character	Text	Text
2. Christ born in the midst of the world's terror	World's terror	Terror
3. Joy/terror mixed together	Mixed world	Mixed
4. "O Little Town of Bethlehem"	Bethlehem	Bethlehem
5. Bethlehem: Cities	Cities	Cities
6. Bethlehem: Nightmare	Nightmare	Nightmare
7. Bethlehem: Darkness	Darkness	Darkness
8. Bethlehem: Fears	Fears	Fears
9. For many, only terror this Christmas	Terror	Terror
10. *St. Elsewhere*	*St. Elsewhere*	*St. Elsewhere*

II. Solution: Jesus – The Victor Over All

IDEA	PICTURE	IMAGE
1. Jesus outlived Herod	Text	Text
2. Foreshadow of the Gospel	Gospel	Gospel
3. Christmas a reminder that Christ is with us	Presence	Presence

155

4. Signs of victory are around us	Victory signs	Victory
5. Danny	Danny	Danny

Conclusion

1. Must leave the dinosaur in the manger	Dinosaur	Dinosaur
2. Herod dies, Jesus lives!	Jesus lives!	Jesus lives!

IMAGE	Sermon Content
Dinosaur	Wes Seeliger, a Methodist minister, told of one of his family events at Christmas. They were making a Christmas manger scene and everybody was putting in animals and the statues of Mary and Joseph and Jesus. As he walked by it once, he did a double-take. His five-year-old boy, Scott, wanting to make his contribution, had put a Tyrannosaurus Rex, a dinosaur, right into the middle of the manger scene. There it stood, so menacing, so terrifying.

Seeliger said that his first reaction was to take it out, but he did not want to hurt Scott's feelings. So he thought he would tell him that the dinosaur was out of date, was extinct by the time of Christ. Or to tell him that it just did not look good, was not very decorative. Then he said, "I caught myself because I realized that, in essence, he had caught the truth of Christmas. For Christmas came to help us face the dinosaurs life places before us – those menacing terrors that seem to be so strong, so powerful. Christmas came to defeat them."[1]

Herod — I can understand his reaction. When I came in and saw that dinosaur standing in the middle of this manger scene on the table, I wanted to take it out. It shouldn't be there! I want angels and shepherds and wisemen and Mary and Joseph and the baby – all the nice images in the story. Maybe you felt that way as you saw it today. But the more I thought about it, I think Seeliger was right. We have to leave it there. For this dinosaur symbolizes terror, and pain, and suffering and death. And as much as we do not want to think about it, it is a vital part of our Christmas story. For the truth is, I think there was a dinosaur in the Christmas story – and its name was Herod.

I. Problem: Herod – The Terror We Face.

Remember Herod? Matthew puts him right in the middle of the Christmas story. As I read about him, I wanted to rip that part out of the story. Then it would be so pretty, with angels and a star and shepherds and all. But I can not take him out. He is there and we are going to have to deal with him. Herod – quite a character!

– Herod, the evil one. He killed his family to stay in power. Did you know that he had an order passed that on the day of his death, the leading citizens of Jerusalem would be killed so that there would be mourning in Jerusalem when he died?

– Herod, the liar. He wanted to come and worship the baby. What a laugh!

– Herod, the insecure. Think of it. Mighty king, powerful one, trembling at the thought of the birth of a tiny, helpless baby.

– Herod, the murderer. He sent soldiers to kill all the boy babies two years and under. Think about that! Because Christ was born, innocent children died and parents cried. And the prophecy was fulfilled: "A voice was heard in Ramah, wailing and loud lamentation, Rachel weeping for her children; She refused to be consoled, because they were no more" (Matthew. 2:18).

What a terrible "dinosaur" Herod was. How we wish he wasn't there, but he is. And I think he is there to remind us that Jesus was not born into an antiseptic world, cleansed of all the dirt and grime that sin and evil bring. He was born right into the middle of it, and He had to struggle against the terror and the pain and the suffering and the death, just like everyone else. It would not be easy for Jesus to survive in the world.

Mixed

Our world is not so different. Dinosaurs and Herods still walk our streets, bringing terror and struggle. Many of the people we seek to minister to this Christmas will have a hard time singing, "Joy to the World." Life has been hard on them. They know only pain and heartbreak. So we will celebrate joy and hope and love and grace. But many will only see the Herods and all the terrors that come along with him. It is all mixed together. Joy, but also sorrow. Hope, but also despair. Love, but also hate. Do we understand that? It is not an easy time for many.

Bethlehem

So we will sing, "O Little Town of Bethlehem, how still we see thee lie."

Cities

But our Bethlehems, our cities, are far from still. The stillness is broken by:
– The sounds of the homeless shuffling about, trying to find a place to sleep.
– The sounds of gunshots and the screams of fear as many struggle just to survive another day in their ghettos of poverty.
– The cries of the drug addicts and the alcoholics and the desperate seeking to make it through the pain of the day.

Nightmare

So we sing on. "Above thy deep and dreamless sleep, the silent stars go by." For many, not sleep, but nightmares of:
– Wars that never seem to end and leave too many innocent people dead.
– Prejudice that divides people on the basis of race, gender, nation, denomination.
– The powerful who oppress the poor while feathering their own nest.

Darkness

We sing, "Yet in thy dark streets shineth, the Everlasting Light." But many do not see the

159

light. They see only the darkness, the darkness:

– Of sin that leads to pain and suffering.

– Of evil that leads to hate and despair.

– Of death that leads to hopelessness and emptiness.

Fears We finish, "The hopes and fears of all the years are met in thee tonight." Many do not see the hope, they only see the fears:

– Fear of cancer, heart disease, and AIDS.

– Fear of each other, of war, of violence.

– Fear of meaninglessness, of rejection, of loneliness, of being a nobody.

So it is in our world. The Herods still threaten the manger and the hope God sent in Jesus. As we preach and teach and seek to minister to the hurts of people, may we never forget how hard it will be for some to see the hope and feel the joy. How will we help them face their dinosaurs?

St. Elsewhere There was a television series years ago called *St. Elsewhere*. It concerned the activities of doctors and nurses in a Boston hospital. One of the main characters was Dr. Craig, a leading heart surgeon. He was always the prim and proper one, acting like he had his life all in order. But he had a son that he could not get along with and one night after a violent argument, the son drives away in anger and has a car wreck and is killed. When Dr. Craig finds out about it, he sheds no tears. "That's the way life goes," he says, "and we must get along with our lives." No grief at all, no seeming pain.

It is Christmas Eve, and there is the customary party at his house. In the kitchen, for the first time he lets out his pain. He cries out, "How could God do this to me? I don't deserve it! It's not right! It's not fair!"

160

There is a Christmas Eve service. His wife and family go to it. Even his agnostic friend, Dr. Westfall, goes, seeking to give God a chance this night. But Dr. Craig would not go. In the last scene, you see the church, hear the Christmas music coming from inside, and you see Dr. Craig making his way through the falling snow, climbing up the steps of the church. He stands at the door and listens. You can see the struggle on his face. Would he go in and hold on to God, in spite of all the pain he was in? What would he do? The last sight you see is Dr. Craig, walking back down the steps, going out alone into the dark night. This Christmas, no room for God!

For many, this is the way it is this Christmas. Maybe it is this way for you. There are just too many Herods, too much terror. It is a dark world for them. Is there a word we have for them?

Solution Text   II. Solution: Jesus – The Victor Over All.

We need to follow the story all the way through. Herod chased after Jesus, but Mary and Joseph fled to Egypt. The soldiers could not catch Him. Even with all the power and might of the Roman government behind him, Herod was no match for the protection of God over the child. Then, almost matter-of-factly, the scripture said, "But when Herod died." What irony! Here was Herod, powerful, mighty, king! And here was Jesus, tiny, helpless, dependent on others. Guess who wins! Herod dies, Jesus lives! The dinosaur, as powerful and terrifying as it was, was not strong enough to stop what God had done.

Gospel   So here in this Christmas story, we have a foreshadowing of the gospel. "Herod dies, Jesus lives!" All through His life, the Herods would

161

chase after Jesus. Finally one Friday, they caught Him. They put Him on a cross and crucified Him. But even there, the message of Christmas was heard again. "Herod dies, Jesus lives!" God raised Jesus from the dead. Herod threw everything he had at Jesus – pain, suffering, death. But it was not enough to stop what God was doing. It never is!

Presence

Here is the reason we need to sing the carols, put on the Christmas pageants, tell the story of the birth again. It is a reminder of the presence of God among us. What God started at Christmas is still going on. It cannot be stopped. God has come to be with us in our struggle against the Herods of life. We are not alone. God is with us! Because that is true, even in the face of terror, we can hold on to hope. God will fight the fight with us. God will help us triumph over our enemies.

Victory

Every now and then, we can get little glimpses of such victories in life. An injustice is righted, some oppression is overcome, some suffering is conquered, a marriage is saved, an alcoholic recovers, a rebellious child comes home, a lost soul is found. Little pictures of the way that it will be one day. For the story of Christmas is a story of the ultimate victory, where good will and peace will reign everywhere, where the lion will lie down by the lamb, and where God's kingdom will be forever. And all will know the truth of Christmas – Herod dies, Jesus lives!

Danny

One of the people who came across my life was a boy named Danny. Through the years as he "grew up" in the church, I got to know him. He was a very likable boy, then a "fun" teenager. But he was one who always had that "look" on his face. You know, the look that makes you

162

wonder what he had been up to now. He was sort of a mischievous fellow. I liked that. But one rainy night, Danny ran his car off a slippery road into a tree and was killed, dead at 16. This was quite a tragedy for his family, the church family, for his school family. It was just a few days before Christmas and mixed among the carols and parties was the fact that Danny was dead. On a cold and dreary day, the day before Christmas Eve, we buried him.

The next day was Sunday, and on the first verse of the opening hymn, down the aisle came Danny's father and step-mother, sister, brother, grandmother, aunt, and uncle. The only place they could find to sit was on the front pew. I had not expected them to come, and when I saw them, it threw me into a quandary. The first sentence of my sermon that day was this: "Christmas is a time for joy." I thought to myself, how can I say that with them sitting there? Should I change the sermon? Well, it was too late for that. But as I thought about it, what I was to say was a needed word for that moment. For I was not going to talk about joy as a "plastic smile" or a "superficial ha-ha." I was going to talk about joy as being a deep confidence in the faithfulness of God to finish what was started in Bethlehem. Since Jesus came, we can live with the deep joy of knowing that all that terrifies and hurts us will one day be destroyed. And that means that what we did in that cemetery the day before was not the final word about anything.

The service ended. Danny's father came by, and with a tear streaming down his cheek, took my hand and said, "It really *is* true, isn't it!"

Yes, it *really* is! It really *is*!

163

Conclusion

Dinosaur   As much as I would like to take the dinosaur out of the manger, I have decided to leave it there. It is a reminder of the way things are. Pain and suffering and struggle and death are still with us. We have to fight them still.

Jesus lives!   But because of Christmas, I know that one day, I can take the dinosaur out. It will be gone forever. What God intends, will come to pass. We are not alone. God is in the struggle with us and will never stop fighting for us until the victory is won.

So here is the word we have to speak this Christmas. Here is the Christmas message. Dinosaurs are extinct! Herod dies, Jesus lives! That which God has started will come to be! For that reason, no matter how hard and difficult life is now, it can always be a very, merry Christmas!

---

1. James Flamming, "Preaching Resources for Special Ocasions," *Proclaim* (Oct.-Dec.), 1976, 39.

Sermon 3: The Front Of The Line

This sermon was an attempt to preach a narrative sermon patterned after the style presented by Eugene Lowry in his book, *The Homiletical Plot*.[1] There are five "signposts" to this sermon, organized according to the divisions given by Lowry.[2] Again, this sermon was preached to seminary students in a chapel service at the North American Baptist Seminary.

COVER PAGE

Title: The Front of the Line

Text: Matthew 20:1-16

CIT: God offered grace freely to all.

Thesis: God offers us grace to be in the kingdom.

GO: Consecrative

SO: That they will celebrate God's grace in their lives.

Signposts:

   I. Upsetting the Equilibrium (oops)

  II. Analyzing the Discrepancy (ugh)

 III. Disclosing the Clue to Resolution (aha)

 IV. Experiencing the Gospel (whee)

  V. Anticipating the Consequences (yeah)

IMAGE OUTLINE

IDEA	PICTURE	IMAGE
I. Upsetting the Equilibrium (oops)		
1. Familiar parable	Parable	Parable
2. Seems God is unfair	Unfair	Unfair
II. Analyzing the Discrepancy (ugh)		
1. Parable of the landowner	Text	Text
2. Problem: same wages for all	Wages	Wages
3. Seemed unfair to some workers	Unfair	Unfair
4. We complain how God is unfair to us	Complaints	Complaints
5. God gave what was promised	Fair	Fair
6. Still seems unfair	Unfair	Unfair
III. Disclosing the Clue to Resolution (aha)		
1. Why do we feel we are at the back of the line?	Back	Back
2. Place for us is at the front	Front	Front
3. Grace given to all possible	Grace	Grace
IV. Experiencing the Gospel (whee)		
1. Ashby Shaw	Ashby	Ashby
2. Never lost the wonder of grace	"Amazing"	"Amazing"

V. Anticipating the Consequences (yeah)

1. Where is our place in   Our place   Place
   line?
2. Celebrate our life in   Celebrate grace   Celebrate
   grace
3. Where are we?   Where?   Where?

IMAGE	Sermon Content

I. Oops

Parable

Well, there it is. Another one of the parables of Jesus. We like the parables, nice little stories that often have powerful and surprising insights into the kingdom of God. They are interesting to read and discuss.

Unfair

But we have to admit that there is something about this parable that disturbs us. Something seems to be wrong about this one. Dare we say it? Somehow in this parable, God seems – unfair!

II. Ugh

Text

What's going on here? Here's the background. Jesus had been talking about how tough it would be for rich people to get into the kingdom. Peter asked, "We've left everything to follow you. What will we get?" So Jesus told this story.

A householder went out early in the morning to hire people to work in his vineyard. Now we understand that the householder represents God, the vineyard is the kingdom, and the workers – they are all of us. So he hired workers for a fair wage. He went out several times to find workers, even going out just one hour before quitting time to hire some more workers.

Wages

The day ended and the time came to pay the workers. He had them line up. Those who had worked the longest were at the back of the line, those who had worked only one hour were put at the front of it. He paid them first and gave to them – a denarius! That's what he had promised to pay the first workers. When those at the back of the line saw that, they began to murmur among themselves. "Did you see that?" Their mental calculators went to work. "Why, we should get 10 or 12 denarii!" They were full of anticipation. But when they got their wages, it was only one denarius. They were not happy. They began to grumble and complain. "It's not fair! We worked all day in the hot sun. They only worked one hour. We should get more than they did. It's just not fair!"

Complaints

And we say "amen" to that. We identify with them. They *had* worked harder and done more. It wasn't fair. Here's the principle: the more you do, the more you give, the more you should get. Deep down, this is the way we feel about discipleship. It is the way our people feel about it. None of us may admit it, but it is the way we feel.

– "I don't understand it. I have gone to church all my life. I've tried to be a good Christian. I don't understand why I should get sick when that man who never goes to church hasn't been sick a day of his life."

– "I live honestly, decently. I try to do what is right. Why did God let that other person get that job promotion? Why, they are not that honest!"

– "We've come to seminary. We've suffered through Hebrew and Greek and preaching. We have made a lot of sacrifices to come here. How come God doesn't give us a good church to serve in?"

Fair

It does not seem fair! What does the householder say? He asks a question. "How much did I promise to pay you?" "A denarius." "How much did I give you?" "A denarius." "So, what's the problem? I did for you what I

169

promised, didn't I?" "Yes, you did," they said. But under their breath, they still murmured, "It still isn't fair!"

God turns to us and asks us. "Did I promise you that if you went to church and were a good Christian that you wouldn't get sick?" "Well, no." "Did I promise you that if you lived decently, you were guaranteed that job promotion?" "Uh, no." "Did I promise you that if you went into the ministry, that I would give you big churches and plush ministries?" "No, you didn't. But . . ."

Unfair

God has done for us what was promised. We can't argue with that. But still – it seems so unfair!

III. Aha

Back

What do we make of all this! Maybe we have put ourselves in the wrong place in the parable. Why is it that we always put ourselves at the back of the line? Do we think we deserve to be there? Those at the back of the line had worked harder and done more than the others. Do we feel that is our situation? Have we done more than most? But God has been at this business of building the kingdom for a long time. I know that there have been a lot of others who have worked in the kingdom who have done a whole lot more and given a whole lot more than we have. So why do we think this is where we are standing?

Front

Maybe where we are meant to be in this parable is at the front of the line. Those at the front of the line knew that they had gotten what they did not deserve or could not earn. Instead, they had gotten undeserved blessings. They had gotten – grace! This was the way of the householder, always going out, trying to find others that he could bring in. Peter wanted to know what they would get for following Jesus. "You get the kingdom. Isn't that enough? Isn't that what you need?" They were "in" – they had gotten grace! Those at the front of the line didn't question God's fairness. One thing they knew. God was more than fair. God was "graceful."

Grace

This is where we are meant to be. At the front of the line. We have gotten an invitation to be part of God's kingdom. We did not deserve it. We could never earn our way in. But it doesn't matter. God has come to us with grace. God gives to us what we do not deserve and could never earn, but what we desperately need. Isn't that overwhelming? Isn't that exciting? We are "in!" Grace has come to us. Don't we stand in awe of that?

IV. Whee

Ashby

Ashby Shaw was a dynamic Christian whom I met during my service in a church in my college years. He had been involved in a construction accident and had been in the hospital for three months. During that time, Ashby was converted to Christ through a Billy Graham crusade on television.

The first time I met him, he asked me, "Do you know what's amazing?" "No, what?" "Isn't it amazing that God loves you and me?" "Yes, it is." The second time I saw him, he asked, "You know what's amazing?" "What?" "Isn't it amazing that God loves you and me?" The third time I saw him, I said, "Yes, Ashby, I know that it's amazing that God loves you and me." "Isn't it?" he said. That was the way Ashby was. After a while, I was jumping over tables and chairs to

171

try to avoid him. But if there was anyone who truly understood this parable, Ashby was the one. He never got over the amazement of being allowed to be a part of the kingdom of God. He never lost his wonder over God's grace. And his life was a testimony to that truth. Every day was exciting for him, a gift of grace from the hand of God.

"Amazing"   Well, isn't it amazing? We have been given what we don't deserve, what we cannot earn. We have been given grace to enter the kingdom. We need that. God has turned and given it to us.

V. Yeah

Place   So here is the sum of it. Those at the back of the line are always complaining about what they didn't get, what others have gotten. As a result, they never enjoy what they do have. But those at the front of the line – they are having a celebration. They know what grace is, because they had gotten it. They didn't deserve it. Couldn't earn it. But no matter! Because of God's grace, they were in the kingdom, enjoyers of the blessings of God.

Celebrate   Would it make a difference in our lives if we lived them as gifts of grace? Maybe we would celebrate the privilege that is ours to be allowed to come to seminary and study the sacred matters of God. Maybe we would complain less about the responsibilities we have and celebrate the grace that gives us such responsibilities. Maybe life would be more joyful to us if we realized that every day we live it is *because* of the grace of God, *in* the grace of God, *through* the grace of God. Maybe we would celebrate the wonder of the marvelous grace given to us.

172

Where?   Do we know what is amazing? We always
                          do, we always do, if we remember where we are
                          standing. Right there! Right there – at the front
                          of the line!

---

1. Eugene Lowry, *The Homiletical Plot* (Atlanta: John Knox
Press, 1980).

2. *Ibid.*, 25.

SELECTED BIBLIOGRAPHY

Of the writing of books or preaching, there seems to be no end. I am presenting a very limited bibliography of books on preaching that have proved helpful to me. Not all of them touch on the subject at hand, but they do share some incisive insights into preaching that are helpful.

Achtemeir, Elizabeth. *Preaching from the Old Testament.* Louisville: Westminster/John Knox Press, 1984.

Bausch, William. *Storytelling: Imagination and Faith.* Mystic, CT: Twenty-Third Publications, 1984.

Brown, David M. *Dramatic Narrative in Preaching.* Valley Forge: Judson Press, 1981.

Brueggemann, Walter. *Finally Comes the Poet: Daring Speech for Proclamation.* Minneapolis: Fortress, 1989.

Buechner, Frederick. *Telling the Truth.* San Francisco: Harper and Row, 1977.

Buttrick, David. *Homiletic.* Philadelphia: Fortress, 1987.

Claypool, John. *The Preaching Event.* Waco, TX: Word Books, 1980.

Cox, James. *Preaching.* San Francisco: Harper and Row, 1985.

Craddock, Fred. *Overhearing the Gospel.* Nashville: Abingdon Press, 1978.

_____. *Preaching.* Nashville: Abingdon Press, 1988.

Eslinger, Richard L., ed. *Intersections: Post-Critical Studies in Preaching.* Grand Rapids: William B. Eerdmans Publishing Company, 1994.

_____. *A New Hearing.* Nashville: Abingdon Press, 1987.

Fant, Clyde E. *Preaching for Today.* San Francisco: Harper and Row, 1987.

Fasol, Al. *A Guide to Self-Improvement in Delivery.* Grand Rapids: Baker Book House, 1983.

Freeman, Harold. *Variety in Biblical Preaching.* Waco, TX: Word Books, 1987.

Hostetler, Michael. *Illustrating the Sermon.* Grand Rapids: Zondervan Publishing House, 1989.

Howard, J. Grant. *Creativity in Preaching.* Grand Rapids: Zondervan Publishing House, 1987.

Jensen, Richard A. *Telling the Story.* Minneapolis: Augsburg Publishing House, 1980.

_____. *Thinking in Story.* Lima, OH: CSS Publishing Co., 1993.

Koller, Charles. *Expository Preaching Without Notes.* Grand Rapids: Baker Book House, 1962.

Lewis, Ralph with Gregg Lewis. *Inductive Preaching.* Westchester, IL: Crossway Books, 1976.

Long, Thomas. *Preaching and the Literary Forms of the Bible.* Philadelphia: Fortress Press, 1989.

_____. *The Witness of Preaching.* Louisville: Westminster/John Knox Press, 1989.

Lowry, Eugene L. *The Homiletical Plot.* Atlanta: John Knox Press, 1980.

_____. *Doing Time in the Pulpit.* Nashville: Abingdon Press, 1985.

_____. *How to Preach a Parable.* Nashville: Abingdon Press, 1989.

Macartney, Clarence E. *Preaching Without Notes.* Nashville: Abingdon Press, 1946.

Mitchell, Henry. *Celebration and Experience in Preaching.* Nashville: Abingdon Press, 1990.

Muehl, William. *Why Preach? Why Listen?* Philadelphia: Fortress Press, 1986.

Rice, Charles. *The Embodied Word.* Minneapolis: Fortress Press, 1991.

Robinson, Wayne Bradley, ed. *Journeys Toward Narrative Preaching.* New York: The Pilgrim Press, 1990.

Rogness, Michael. *Preaching to a TV Generation.* Lima, OH: CSS Publishing Company, 1994.

Salmon, Bruce C. *Storytelling in Preaching.* Nashville: Broadman Press, 1988.

Sanders, James A. *God Has a Story Too.* Philadelphia: Fortress Press, 1979.

Shoemaker, H. Stephen. *Retelling the Biblical Story.* Nashville: Broadman Press, 1985.

Smith, Christine M. *Weaving the Sermon.* Louisville: Westminster/ John Knox Press, 1989.

Steimle, Edmund; Niedenthal, Morris; and Rice, Charles. *Preaching the Story.* Philadelphia: Fortress Press, 1980.

Swank, George W. *Dialogic Style in Preaching.* Valley Forge: Judson Press, 1981.

Thulin, Richard L. *The "I" of the Sermon.* Minneapolis: Fortress Press, 1988.

Troeger, Thomas H. *Creating Fresh Images for Preaching.* Valley Forge: Judson Press, 1982.

_____. *Imagining a Sermon.* Nashville: Abingdon Press, 1990.

Vines, Jerry. *A Guide to Effective Sermon Delivery.* Chicago: Moody Press, 1986.

Wardlow, Don M., ed. *Preaching Biblically.* Philadelphia: Westminster Press, 1981.

Willimon, William. *Integrative Preaching.* Nashville: Abingdon Press, 1988.

_____. *Peculiar Speech.* Grand Rapids: William B. Eerdmans Publishing Company, 1992.

_____; Steve Brown; and Haddon Robinson. *A Voice in the Wilderness.* Sisters, OR: Multnomah Press, 1993.

Wilson, Paul Scott. *Imagination of the Heart.* Nashville: Abingdon Press, 1988.

Wilson-Kastner, Patricia. *Imagery for Preaching.* Minneapolis: Fortress Press, 1989.